Stirring Up Justice

Writing and Reading to Change the World

Jessica Singer

HEINEMANN ■ Portsmouth, NH

Heinemann
A division of Reed Elsevier Inc.
361 Hanover Street
Portsmouth, NH 03801–3912
www.heinemann.com

Offices and agents throughout the world

Library of Congress Cataloging-in-Publication Data
Singer, Jessica.
    Stirring up justice : writing and reading to change the world / Jessica Singer.
        p. cm.
    Includes bibliographical references.
    ISBN 0-325-00747-0 (alk. paper)
    1. Social action—Study and teaching (Secondary)—United States. 2. Social justice—Study and teaching (Secondary)—United States.   I. Title.

HN65.S5625 2006
303.48′4071273—dc22   2006000561

Editor: Tom Newkirk
Production: Vicki Kasabian
Cover design: Joni Doherty, based on a design by Jake Early
Typesetter: Tom Allen, Pear Graphic Design
Manufacturing: Steve Bernier

Printed in the United States of America on acid-free paper
10 09 08 07 06 ML 1 2 3 4 5

For Rose Horowitz

This is for your coffee table

ontents

Acknowledgments

This book would not have existed without Ruth Shagoury. Ruth has been my professor, advisor, mentor, research colleague, writing partner, and dear friend for the last decade. I have never met anyone who more understands the role of a mentor. She selflessly creates opportunities for her students to collaborate with her and learn to become researchers, activists, and remarkable educators. This book is an example of the fruits of her mentorship. She is always generous with her time and support, and I admire her continued direct involvement in classrooms with teachers and her work as an activist educator. Ruth exemplifies to me the integration of academic study for direct benefits in the educational life of students. I want to thank Linda Christensen and Bill Bigelow for being exemplary educators committed to teaching for social justice. I want to thank my students at Cleveland High School for their willingness to embrace this work, their good humor, and their passionate writing and art. Thanks to Harriet Wingard for Saturday mornings at the Pearl Bakery and for collaboration. To Sheridan Blau, my advisor—thank you for your support. My gratitude to Tom Newkirk, my editor, for teaching me that writing is an opportunity to "take a turn" in a conversation. Thank you for helping me to take my turn. To Gus, thank you for being with me throughout this journey. To Kenny, Malia, Matt, Jenna, and Sophie Rose, much love. To Mom and Dad, my gratitude for your friendship, support, teaching, and kindness. The value you place on education is my inspiration. Thank you, Mom, for always being my first reader and editor. To Jake Early, your talent as an artist, photographer, and graphic designer are all a piece of this book. Thanks for listening over phone lines, Illy coffee, and waves at Mondos.

Introduction

My connection to other Oregon educators committed to teaching social justice influenced my interest in social activism. As an active member of Portland Area Rethinking Schools, a local and national progressive activist group for educators, I was surrounded by an incredible group of teachers creating innovative curricula and working to influence progressive change in local schools. Though I have never considered myself a traditional activist or political organizer, I have strong convictions—particularly about the need for creating more equity in education and more creative opportunities for all students to learn. I participated in the Portland Area Rethinking Schools Steering Committee, a group of new and experienced teachers, parents, and community members. Our conversations and work together gave me courage to start thinking about the kind of change I wanted to take place at my school.

Cleveland is a large public school located on the corner of a busy intersection in the heart of the city. The student population is just under 1,400, and 20 percent of the student body qualifies for either free or reduced-price lunches. My students were from a working-class population, with about 25 percent speaking a language other than English as their first language. The school's student body, much like the state of Oregon, is predominately Caucasian (77 percent). Students arrived in my classes with varying reading and writing skills ranging from barely literate to highly proficient. One of the first things I noticed was the way students were divided into two groups: "honors" and "regulars." Honors was the name assigned to all classes where students earned honors credit by taking the class; regular classes were those considered less challenging and that moved at a slower pace. The content in these classes was not parallel. I had previously taught for a year in a public, untracked, international high school in Oregon. I had never taught in a tracked system, and I was naïve about the divisions, assumptions, and learning cultures created and perpetuated through tracking.

My own activism project began when I decided to work with my English department to untrack our ninth grade course offerings. Instead of having freshmen begin their high school language arts studies sorted and segregated in courses, previously labeled "honors" and "regulars," I worked along with my department members to implement a system of learning where students were no longer divided by earlier success or failure. Rather than beginning some students at a more accelerated level than others, we were committed to offering everyone a chance to receive an "honors" education and begin high school English with a clean slate. I experienced firsthand what it is like to believe in a cause so strongly that I felt driven. I spent the majority of my free evenings working to research and educate myself about untracking, meeting with my department, and planning ways of making this change take place successfully. After two years working toward this goal, our department decided unanimously to untrack our ninth grade classes and to work toward eventually untracking all of our course offerings, at every grade level.

For the first time in my school's history, English teachers were preparing to teach courses where students with different academic, ethnic, and social class backgrounds would be learning together. One of the main challenges teaching any group of students, and one that I knew would be accentuated teaching untracked courses, is that students have a wide array of learning needs. With this in mind, I wanted to find a way to capture my students' interest by making learning both exhilarating and rewarding. I also wanted to teach a curriculum that would reach all of my students, whether or not they considered themselves strong readers and writers. Through my own activism work, I became interested in finding ways for my students to experience the kind of drive and passion that comes when studying topics they care about deeply. I wanted students to experience the powerful relevance of reading and writing by exploring their own convictions.

I began to wonder about their interests and passions. What did they care deeply about? What issues and ideas mattered so much to them that they could be inspired to act? Teaching a truly diverse community is both challenging and rewarding. There was

Danika, who at fifteen was five feet seven inches tall and a varsity soccer player. Her writing was often poetic and full of voice. She rarely misplaced a comma or a quotation mark. She wrote notes at the end of papers asking for book recommendations—"preferably classics." Then there was Nate. He signed his name "N8." He was fourteen years old and obsessed with skateboarding. He read and wrote well below grade level. He rarely formed complete sentences and often seemed distracted and worried. There was Jeff. He was six feet two inches tall and wore jeans that sagged below the hip. He loved Air Jordans, hip-hop music, and looking cool. He often refused to carry his books in the halls and left them in a cupboard in the classroom. His writing seemed natural and confident, though sometimes scattered. He was usually the first to have his hand up and the last to put it down. Jeff said, "I hate to revise. Revising is for people with too much time. I'm always in a hurry." There was shy Paul who read poetry and listened to music on his Walkman. He often arrived late because he cared for his younger brother in the mornings. There was Erik, who has Asbergers syndrome. He methodically drew ships and hallways on blank paper before class. He listened to pop music and befriended Emma. Emma loved to paint canvases full of bright flowers and write letters to her pen pal in Argentina. Students in these classes came from a cross section of southeast Portland that includes neighborhoods of extreme wealth and extreme poverty. These ninth graders did not easily fit into neat categories or definitions. They did not all clearly fit into a particular "level" or benchmark. Arriving at my class in different places in their literacy development and their lives, what these students needed in their learning was complicated and without easy explanation. I created the Stirring Up Justice curriculum to provide multiple perspectives for students to understand and define activism.

Thinking about the activism unit, I began with high hopes. At first, I had visions of my ninth graders out in the community creating social change, perhaps even working on one project together. My ideas about activism initially followed the more narrow and traditional view of activism. When thinking about activists and their work, I often imagined individuals marching with signs in protests, drafting petitions, taking up environmental causes, organizing rallies, and partaking in other stereotypical antiestablishment behavior. Through developing and teaching this unit, I came to understand that there is a wide range of socially active behavior that falls well beyond the more common perception of activism.

I went on a walk with a friend early in October when I had just begun planning the Stirring Up Justice unit. I shared my plans to teach a unit at the end of the school year on activism. My friend suggested that the entire class work toward an issue "like the recent janitor cuts in Oregon or the school funding crisis." Something in this conversation did not sit right with me. True leaders and activists have skills carefully honed over time, and do not instantly become sincere and effective activists as the result of one classroom assignment. They have passions that stem from their own particular life experience. I wanted this curriculum to create opportunities for students' individual interests and multiple perspectives to enter the classroom discourse, rather than forcing my own agenda. Paulo Freire explains this distinction eloquently: "A humane educator's fundamental objective is to fight alongside the people for the recovery of the people's humanity, not to 'win people over' to their side" (1970, 84). I continually asked myself, "How can I set the agenda for what my students should care about? I want my role to be as a guide and to give my students a backdrop to begin to explore issues that matter to them."

This book shares a long journey I took with my students to choose an issue they each cared about and then to guide them through working toward creating positive social change surrounding their individual interests. By sharing their individual projects as they prepared them in and out of class, students also learned that activism is not a solo process and that influencing change grows with support and camaraderie. Using a range of literacy tools—including reading biographies of activists, creating gallery displays, writing essays, revising written work, interviewing activists, and teaching other class members—the students learned the power of using their literacy to make positive changes in the world.

Nuts and Bolts

In the beginning of the school year, months before I introduced the unit on activism, I taught literature and short stories from

South Africa along with the history of political efforts to abolish apartheid. Students read Mark Mathabane's autobiography, *Kaffir Boy* (1986), along with short stories from other South African writers such as Peter Abrahams, Nadine Gordimer, and Doris Lessing. Next I taught Latin American literature, where students explored issues of family, identity, and immigration. Along with international literature, students read multiple texts about traditionally marginalized groups in the United States. Throughout the year, students explored literature and history from a variety of cultures while simultaneously participating in writing and reading workshops that provided skills for understanding difficult texts and writing in multiple genres.

Each project, text, and area of study during the initial months of the school year built up to the final three-month unit on social activism described in this book. Before students participated in the activism unit, they were exposed to a variety of stories about people committed to effecting positive social change. This is in no way a requirement for teaching this curriculum; however, it did add to students' preparedness for the final unit. Creating curriculum throughout the year that highlighted political or inspirational activists was not difficult. Much of the required literature or literature "in-stock" in high schools includes rich stories of people devoted to making a difference in others' lives. I included texts such as Sandra Cisneros' *House on Mango Street* (1991), Gail Tsukiyama's *The Samurai's Garden* (1995), and Melba Beals' *Warriors Don't Cry* (1994). My reading curriculum fluctuated back and forth between required texts that the whole class read together and books students chose revolving around specific themes such as immigration, apartheid in South Africa, and social activism. The two ninth-grade classes read a total of five required books during the year in addition to at least four books of choice. As students read, they also worked directly with me and with each other to improve as writers. The continual integration and scaffolding of direct reading and writing instruction provided a foundation for students to succeed in the last three months of spring term with the culminating social activism unit.

In the beginning of April, I began this final Stirring Up Justice unit. I established a schedule where, for the most part, reading workshops and reading skill development took place on Monday, Wednesday, and Fridays; writing workshops and writing skill development took place on Tuesday and Thursday. My high school operates on a partial block schedule, meaning that twice a week (Tuesday and Thursday) classes are ninety minutes long, while on the other days they are forty-eight minutes long. A typical reading or writing workshop day began with me teaching or modeling a reading or writing strategy such as rereading difficult passages for improved understanding or weaving quotes effectively into writing. A whole class reading or writing activity followed so students could practice the specific strategy taught that day. Students then often shared their work in groups or as a class. Setting up a routine schedule each week helped students arrive at class aware of the day's focus. A series of short writing workshops in the beginning of the unit connected to students' assigned reading provided scaffolding for students to later write articles about the activists they had studied. I informed students from the beginning of the unit and reminded them throughout the course of the curriculum that the work they were doing in April and May would help them succeed in creating their own activism projects in June. At the end of the year, students shared their final activism projects in a gallery format during the last week of the school year (see Appendix 1: Unit Timeline).

Portfolios

Finding a way to read, assess, and manage the hundreds of pages of writing that came my way in a week became an essential piece of my teaching and planning. I set up a portfolio system with my students that helped all of us stay organized and gave me a way to handle their work successfully. At the beginning of each unit, I handed students a piece of paper labeled "Table of Contents," with numbers listed down the side. (See a sample in Appendix 2.) I also required that each student bring a portfolio folder to class (the kind with the brackets that allows the paper to stay fastened within the folder) at the beginning of the unit. I always bought extra folders for students who did not have access to these school supplies. As students completed work of any kind, they added assignments to their table of contents and then included them in order in their portfolios. Often portfolios are used in teaching to show a finished product that exemplifies a writer's or artist's best work. In contrast, I wanted my students' portfolios to represent their rough as well as their polished work. I am interested in their progress and development as readers and writers over the course of a unit. I also taped a large piece of poster paper on the wall and used it as a "Master Table of Contents." Students could walk into class each day and update their portfolios. This system helped all of us stay organized and assisted students who missed class for any reason in catching up with the course work. I collected portfolios every two weeks to read, respond to, and grade.

My hope is that this book provides a window into my classroom along with offering concrete and practical resources for secondary language arts teachers and teacher educators. I have included the kinds of handouts, book lists, student examples, and stories that I would have liked at my fingertips when I began teaching this curriculum. My wish is that teachers open up this book to utilize, revise, and improve upon any idea that feels useful to their own work. My intention is to share resources, processes, and student outcomes in order to paint a clear picture of a classroom in action.

References

Beals, M. 1994. *Warriors Don't Cry: A Searing Battle to Integrate Little Rock's Central High School.* New York: Pocket Books.

Cisneros, S. 1991. *The House on Mango Street.* Houston, TX: Arte Publico Press.

Friere, P. 1970. *Pedagogy of the Oppressed.* New York: Herder and Herder.

Mathabane, M. 1995. *Kaffir Boy: The True Story of a Black Youth's Coming of Age in Apartheid South Africa.* New York: Random House.

Tsukiyama, G. 1995. *The Samurai's Garden.* New York: St. Martin's Press.

1 Stories of Justice
Collaborative Writing

Tikvah means hope and hope is repre-
sented by children. It is they who must
justify our hope in education, human rela-
tions, and social justice. In other words:
they represent our hope in a future, which
is an improvement on our past.

—Elie Wiesel, *Tikvah*

In his edited collection of poems, *Poetry Like Bread*, Martin Espada writes, "Any progressive social change must be imagined first, and that vision must find its most eloquent possible expression to move from vision to reality. Any oppressive social condition, before it can be changed, must be named and condemned in words that persuade by stirring the emotions, awakening the senses" (2000, 16). I love what Espada hints at here about the role of imagination. If individuals are to change conditions they disagree with, then they must use imagination to invent and shape the kind of world they want to live in. I also believe that it takes models and practice to learn to take risks or to step outside of common expectations. It would be unfair and unethical of me to expect students to want to become activists or to fight for causes that fit my own interests and political agenda. Rather I wanted students to learn about the kinds of skills, literacy practices, support networks, and issues that influence individuals committed to making change in the world. Students were given freedom throughout this unit to choose the activists and issues they studied based on what resonated with their own interests.

The focus of this book's curriculum is on how high school students can use reading and writing to learn about and participate as agents of change. Rather than studying how suffering and wrongdoing are perpetuated, students learned to become activists. They began first by writing about difficult personal experiences with unjust behavior in order to understand how individuals' past actions could have been altered to lead to more positive outcomes. The reading and writing workshops introduced in this first chapter took place with my ninth-grade English classes over a two-week period and formed a foundation for the longer three-month unit on social activism described over the course of this book. These beginning workshops incorporate both reading and writing opportunities for students to reflect on personal experiences with acts of injustice.

My ninth graders started by reading and analyzing children's books that all included characters committed to activism work of some kind. Students read and analyzed these books as a way to grow more familiar with children's stories as a genre, and then participated in a writing workshop where they wrote and revised their own children's stories about experiences as victims, witnesses, or perpetrators of injustice. Students wrote and revised their stories for publication in a children's collection and then I helped them send their writing to my friend's fifth-grade class for feedback. This project led to a written dialogue between two student populations that represent a cross section of an urban community in Portland, Oregon. Their collaboration illustrates how two different communities of writers can witness, support, and shape one another's writing and thinking through the sharing of personal narratives and written feedback. Students learned to shift their writing voices, edit, and revise as they exchanged revision questions and feedback. Scaffolding instruction and skill development helped prepare students for success with this project and helped build a foundation for the unit as a whole. Safe space and community were continually shaped, reshaped, and practiced through this rigorous work.

Before diving into the activism unit by reading autobiographies about famous activists or creating activism projects of their own, I wanted them to begin recognizing and thinking about alternate possibilities to the kinds of injustices they experienced in their daily lives. So rather than asking them to write about outside experiences and ideas, I invited students to share "insider stories" through personal narratives. Having students write about their personal experiences with injustice was inspired by work Linda Christensen has done as a teacher and curriculum specialist in the Portland public schools. Not only did I want the assignment to give students a personal connection but also to be a possible catalyst for generating ideas for the stories students would later write. Over the course of the semester, we shifted to a wider range of writing genres like persuasive and expository essays, poetry, and imaginative writing. My intention behind this writing project was that students would write and share these pieces so that they could see, name, and understand what happened in a past event with the hope that these painful actions may not be repeated.

Starting with Children's Books

Mary arrived early to first-period class every day and sat at her desk with her nose in a continually changing book. One morning before the bell, she looked up to tell me, "Ms. Singer, I wanna read whatever you think is worthy, but I want ya to know that I prefer mysteries and romance novels over anything serious or depressing." I know that Mary's enthusiasm for reading is not always experienced in the same way by all of my students. Matt, Shawn, and Amanda informed me at the beginning of the year that they would read anything and everything, as long as it is connected in some way to the *Lord of the Rings*. Catherine told me she did not enjoy reading but she wants to get good grades, so she will "get through the books I assign." Crystal told me that she does not read at all: "I hate it. I would rather clean the toilet than read a book." As I absorb the varied and diverse reactions to reading, I became more and more determined to find books to challenge and inspire all of my students. While creating this curriculum, I read any and every book I could find about activism in order to find stories that would resonate with this diverse group of high school students. As I read, I continually asked myself, "How do these stories and ideas relate to my students' interests? How can these stories inform, teach, and model skills and strategies that will help support my students in their work as writers, readers, and change makers?" I wanted to find books that model successful activism work. Good sources for such models are children's picture books and storybooks, especially biographies of people who have made a difference.

I sat on the floor in the children's section of Powell's bookstore (www.powells.com) in northwest Portland and browsed through children's books looking for stories about change makers. I read Antonio Skarmeta's *The Composition* (2000), a story of a boy living in a military dictatorship struggling with whether or not to write what he knows about his parents' resistance work for an essay contest in school. As I read this chilling tale, which is currently banned in Argentina, I was struck by its powerful and haunting message about freedom of speech and resistance. Jeanette Winter's book *The Librarian of Basra* (2004) is a lovely story from Iraq about a librarian who believes in the importance of protecting books during a time of war. After the governor denies her permission to move the books from her library to a safe place, she "takes matters into her own hands [and] secretly, she brings books home every night" to protect them until the war ends and she can bring them to a safe library. These children's books describe and illustrate different forms of activism. There are famous resistance workers, such as Rosa Parks and Martin Luther King fighting for civil rights, and there are also stories that reveal less-known or often-unrecognized activism work such as building playgrounds, parks, and community gardens; resisting gang life; helping the homeless; and using poetry to speak out.

Children's books often address sophisticated and politically charged topics and include many of the qualities of great literature. Such texts are accessible to high school students with various reading interests and practices and also provide opportunities for them to "try on" complicated topics in uncomplicated ways. I searched the school library, public libraries, used and new bookstores, and the bookshelves of friends and family to collect children's texts about activism. This kind of research is one of the things I love most about teaching. I love gathering books, art, poetry, music, and news that connect to the conversation in my classroom. Handout 1.1 is a list of books I collected for this workshop on children's literature and social activism.

This list is far from a complete collection of children's books revolving around issues of social change; however, it served as a wonderful launching pad to begin the reading, discussion, and writing for this unit.

Memoirs, Biographies, and Stories of Social Justice

Adler, D. 1993a. *A Picture Book of Frederick Douglass*. Illus. by S. Byrd. New York: Holiday House.

Adler, D. 1993b. *A Picture Book of Rosa Parks*. Illus. by R. Casilla. New York: Holiday House.

Anaya, R. 2000. *Elegy on the Death of Cesar Chavez*. Illus. by G. Enriquez. El Paso, TX: Cinco Puntos Press.

Anzaldua, G. 1993. *Friends from the Other Side*. San Francisco: Children's Book Press. (A story about responses to Mexican "Illegals" by Chicanos already living in the U.S.)

Bridges, R. 1999. *Through My Eyes*. New York: Scholastic Press. (A true story of a girl's experience with desegregation as a first grader in a formerly all-white school.)

Cooper, F. 1996. *Mandela: From the Life of the South African Statesman*. New York: Puffin/Penguin.

Corpi, L. 1997. *Where Fireflies Dance*. Illus. by M. Reisberg. San Francisco: Children's Book Press. (A bilingual tale showing how each person, like the revolutionary Juan Sebastian, has a destiny to follow.)

Cronon, D. 2000. *Click, Clack, Moo: Cows That Type*. Illus. by B. Lewin. New York: Simon & Schuster. (Disgruntled farm animals become activists.)

Demi. 2001. *Gandhi*. New York: Margaret McElderry.

Feelings, T. 1995. *The Middle Passage: White Ships Black Cargo*. New York: Dial.

Fitzpatrick, M., and G. Whitedeer. 1998. *The Long March: A Famine Gift for Ireland*. Hillsboro, OR: Beyond Words Publishing.

Fleischman, P. 1997. *Seedfolks*. New York: HarperCollins. (Thirteen stories telling of individuals transforming a vacant lot into a community garden.)

Hesse, K. 2004. *The Cats in Krasinski Square*. Illus. by W. Watson. New York: Scholastic Press. (The story of a young girl and a group of abandoned cats who struggle to survive during World War II and become resistance fighters working to save those trapped behind ghetto walls.)

Hopkinson, D. 2002. *Under the Quilt of Night.* Illus. by J. E. Ransome. New York: Simon & Schuster. (A story about the Underground Railroad.)

Joosse, B. 2002. *Stars in the Darkness.* Illus. by G. Christie. San Francisco: Chronicle. (Story of resisting gang life.)

Khan, R. 1998. *The Roses in My Carpets.* Illus. by R. Himler. New York: Holiday House. (An Afghani boy helps his family as a carpet weaver.)

Knight, M., and A. O'Brien. 1996. *Talking Walls: The Stories Continue.* Gardiner, ME: Tilbury House. (An exploration of cultures and inspiring acts.)

Kudlinski, K. 1989. *Rachel Carson: Pioneer of Ecology.* New York: Puffin/Penguin.

Kurusa. 1995. *The Streets Are Free.* Illus. by M. Doppert. New York: Annick Press. (Story of self-reliance and work to build a community playground.)

McGovern, A. 1997. *La senora de la caja de carton.* Illus. by M. Backer. New York: Turtle Books. (Story about homelessness and reaching out.)

Pico, F. 1991. *The Red Comb.* Illus. by M. A. Ordez. Ri Piedras, PR: Ediciones Huracon. (How villagers help runaway slaves start a new life.)

Pinkney, A. 2000. *Let It Shine: Stories of Black Women Freedom Fighters.* Illus. by S. Alcorn. New York: Harcourt.

Polacco, P. 2000. *The Butterfly.* New York: Philomel Books. (Two friends experience prejudice during World War II.)

Ransom, C. 1993. *Listening to Crickets: A Story About Rachel Carson.* Illus. by S. O. Haas. New York: Scholastic.

Rappaport, D. 2000. *Freedom River.* Illus. by B. Collier. New York: Hyperion. (True story of John Parker, an African American businessman who bought his freedom and helped others via the Underground Railroad.)

Rappaport, D. 2001. *Martin's Big Words: The Life of Dr. Martin Luther King, Jr.* Illus. by B. Collier. New York: Hyperion.

Rappaport, D. 2002. *No More! Stories and Songs of Slave Resistance.* Illus. by S. Evans. Cambridge, MA: Candlewick Press.

Ringgold, F. 1995. *My Dream of Martin Luther King.* New York: Dragonfly Books.

Ringgold, F. 1999. *If a Bus Could Talk: The Story of Rosa Parks*. New York: Simon & Schuster.

Rockwell, A. 2000. *Only Passing Through: The Story of Sojourner Truth*. Illus. by R. G. Christie. New York: Alfred A. Knopf.

Rodriguez, L. 1997. *America Is Her Name*. Illus. by C. Vasquez. Willimantic, CT: Curbstone Press. (A young girl discovers the power of poetry.)

Skarmeta, A. 2000. *The Composition*. Illus. by A. Ruano. Buffalo, NY: Groundwood. (A child's perspective living in a repressive society.)

Stevens, N. 1999. *Tikvah: Children's Book Creators Reflect on Human Rights*. New York: Sea Star.

Winter, J. 2004. *The Librarian of Basra: A True Story from Iraq*. San Diego: Harcourt.

Wishinsky, F. 1999. *The Man Who Made Parks: The Story of Park Builder Frederick Law Olmsted*. Illus. by S. Zhang. New York: Tundra.

Handout 1.1 *(continued)*

I brought these books into my classroom and displayed them on a large table in the front of the room. Exhibiting texts in inviting and creative ways serves as a "hook" for many of my reluctant readers. When I visit bookstores to find books for my own reading pleasure, the colorful glossy covers arranged flat on tables often capture my attention. Students are no different. They often ignore the books lined up on shelves in my classroom in "library-like" stacks and, instead, wander over to the rotating displays I acquire from garage sales and used bookstores. The morning of the children's book workshop, students immediately asked about the texts displayed on the front table. Emma, Michelle, Nate, and Danika stood at the front of the room before class browsing through the new titles.

I introduced the workshop by reading aloud Doreen Rappaport's *Martin's Big Words: The Life of Dr. Martin Luther King, Jr.* (2001) to the class. I pointed out how the story shares something in common with all of the children's texts gathered for the workshop because it highlights a person who made conscious choices throughout his life to work toward positive change. This book is also remarkable because of the beautiful collage-like illustrations on every page. Whenever I read books aloud to students there is a remarkable stillness and presence that sweeps over the room. It continues to amaze me how students of all ages love to hear stories told or read aloud and how an evocative tale can capture the undivided attention of an often-squirming room full of more than thirty adolescents. After reading aloud the story about Martin Luther King Jr., I asked the class to take thirty minutes to first choose and then read a few of the books carefully on their own. I then gave the class questions to guide their reading (see Handout 1.2).

Students quietly sifted through the books on the front table and then found chairs, countertops, tabletops, and corners on the floor to sit quietly and read. This workshop exposes students to multiple issues that engage activists' time and energy like building public parks, combating poverty and violence, and fighting for equal rights. It also makes explicit the kinds of strategies and support activists use to accomplish their goals. The handout asked students to participate in close readings of the texts. The questions intentionally asked students to think about some of the key concepts and ideas I planned to cover throughout the unit such as turning points in the lives of activists, support networks, and actions taken in order to create change.

In Matt's response to his children's book titled *Gandhi* (2001) —by Demi—he wrote, "Gandhi takes social action in this story when he leads nonviolent protests and spreads his message of nonviolence and tolerance worldwide. He led the protests that eventually freed India of British rule." Emma wrote the following to describe the characters in *Stars in the Darkness* (2002), written by Barbara Joosse: "The young boy and his mother take social action in this book. They participate in 'Peace Walks' at night with their neighbors. They walk with flashlights at night so the 'bangers stop fightin' and so the night is not so scary."

The last question on Handout 1.2 (#6) looks at the differences and similarities between children's literature and the books students read for pleasure as young adults. This question is meant to initiate thinking about the importance of audience, voice, illustration, and purpose within texts. Emma shared her understanding of the differences between these two types of books: "Children's stories are short and cut to the chase. While young adult stories have excess writing, and it takes longer to get to the point." Crystal declared, "If adult's books had more pictures, I

Children's Book Workshop

Please take the time to read at least two children's books. All children's books in this workshop share a common theme of social action. Somewhere in each of these stories is a character working toward positive change. After you have sampled a few books, choose one that you are drawn to and answer the following questions.

Book Title and Author _____

1. What is this book about? Please explain the plot.

2. What character takes social action? Describe the action this person takes.

3. Please find a place in the story where this character experiences a turning point and quote it below. NOTE: The turning point is the place where the character chooses to work toward change.

4. Who or what acted as an ally or support for this character? How did the character find or receive support?

5. What stands out to you in this book? Or what do you find disturbing or unsatisfying? Be specific (e.g., illustrations, moral, specific lines).

6. What are differences and similarities between the books you often read for pleasure and children's literature?

Due Date: _____

would read them more often!" Students began to pinpoint specific attributes that make up children's books like illustrations and simple word choice. This dialogue preceded a writing workshop where students started to draft their own children's stories.

Writing Toward Change: Activities

> Schools need to provide the opportunity for literate occasions for students to share their experiences, work in social relations that emphasize care and concern for others, to take risks, and to fight for a quality of life in which all human beings benefit. (Giroux 1987, 178)

One of my favorite writers, Terry Tempest Williams, explains that the role of the writer is to witness the world through writing so that healing and change may take place. Williams explains that "bearing witness to both the beauty and the pain of our world is a task I want to be a part of. As a writer, this is my work. By bearing witness, the story that is told can provide healing ground. Through the art of language, the art of story, alchemy can occur. And if we choose to turn our backs, we've walked away from what it means to be human" (2004, 321). I am interested in the way writing stories of injustice can lead to a kind of understanding or recognition of past wrongdoing. One way students can start to develop and define their own understanding of social justice is through self-awareness and reflection about events in their own lives. By recognizing acts of injustice, students gain exposure to alternative ways of behaving in the world.

One of the main things I wanted this curriculum to reveal is that activist work is often something that comes from the inside of an individual through feeling, experience, and conviction. I could have easily chosen a particular activism issue to focus this unit on, like the clear-cutting of old-growth forests or the unhealthy food choices in school cafeterias. The list of things I care about and want to see change goes on and on; however, this is my list, not my students'. I want my classes to have the opportunity to read, write, research, and present their own interests and causes. Through support, education, imagination, and careful planning, activists take their personal experiences and ideals and move outward to inform and influence others. In this writing assignment, students started to think about their own experiences with injustice and considered ways they could have acted differently in order to prevent or alter an unnecessary outcome.

This workshop began with students writing a list of the times in their lives when they either experienced or witnessed acts of injustice. I gave the class a few minutes to brainstorm these memories. Here are a few examples of the topics generated.

Brainstorm List

- An after-school fight
- Intolerance in health class
- Discrimination against teenagers in shopping malls
- Bullying at the skateboard park
- Insensitive cafeteria talk
- Discrimination at Dunkin' Donuts
- Recess bullies
- Cliques
- Sibling rivalry
- Summer camp
- Peer pressure at weekend parties

I asked, "Out of the experiences you have jotted down, which one feels like a story waiting to be told? Try to pick something that still feels relevant, interesting, and vivid in your memory—this will make writing about it much easier." I placed the following prompt on the overhead and invited students to write:

Stories of Injustice Prompt

Write about a time in your life when you witnessed, participated in, or experienced an act of injustice. Describe what happened. Where were you? Include dialogue, internal thoughts, and vivid details. After you describe what happened, provide some insight into why this injustice occurred. If you could press rewind on your life and revisit this experience, what could you do differently to create a positive change?

My students, like most writers, create rough and incomplete first drafts. The first writing workshop is only about generating words to lay the foundation for a larger project. I encourage students to keep their pens or pencils moving for five to eight minutes to see what comes to the page. I give students permission to start and restart, to write what feels like nonsense, and to trust ideas that they find compelling. I often write along with students and share my own rough starts to model how writers do not arrive at perfection instantaneously (or at all). Students were engaged and excited about this topic. One of the things we talked about as a class before writing these stories was how we often hold onto the details and feelings connected to powerful experiences through memory and how helpful it is to capture these details within our stories. Spencer wrote about shopping for cough drops at a grocery store and being accused of shoplifting because he is a Latino teenager who wears baggy clothes:

> I was in the grocery store searching for cough drops when I got the uncomfortable feeling of eyes watching me. I asked myself if it was somebody I knew. I was too shy to say anything, but then I worried that the person would think I was rude. Minutes seemed like hours and my mind grew more and more curious. The eyes seemed to burn a hole in my back. My face got hot and red. I could no longer concentrate on what I was there to buy. Who was staring at me? What was I doing that was worthy of being stared at? I plotted a plan in my head to get a good peek at the lurking eyes . . .

Danika described teasing a girl at summer camp and regretting her cruelty. Jaime shared the mistreatment he experienced at the skateboard park because he was shorter than the majority of the other skaters. Ken described his first day of middle school when he was taunted and ridiculed for being Asian American. These stories were honest and powerful.

Students wrote for fifteen minutes before we began to share "favorite lines" in a read-around. "Favorite lines" are sentences that seem to jump off the page or that feel easy to read aloud. Some lines may stand out because they capture a main idea or feeling from a story, and other lines may be shocking, frustrating, or funny. James shared a few fragments from his piece: "The sun was nowhere to be found on the cool autumn afternoon. The huge soccer field was soaked through from rain the night before. A tangle of soccer cleats had torn up the grass beyond recognition."

Corinne shared the beginning lines from her story: "I didn't want to sit in a boring science class listening to our teacher excitedly throwing her hands around explaining science stuff. The walls were covered in encouraging posters saying things like 'Don't Be a Dummy, Go to School.'" I want to provide students with seemingly endless opportunities to share their words in safe and nonthreatening ways. Asking students to begin by sharing one or two lines from their writing often seems less intimidating than requiring them to read a whole piece aloud. Students sometimes ask to share up to one paragraph, which I encourage as well. Most importantly, this kind of sharing allows every student to participate. As students read their "favorite lines," I remind them to listen for details and writing strategies in each other's pieces that they might want to imitate. For example, I pointed out how James used setting description to paint a picture of the wet soccer field in his story.

Students are relieved to discover that writers glean ideas and strategies from one another and that this is not plagiarism. We talk about how certain writers capture voices and stories that remind us of our own. In contrast, there are also voices that feel distant and help remind us of what we are not. I share notes and suggestions I have received over the years from trusted friends, editors, and writing classmates. One note that still means a great deal to me was scribbled by a friend on a piece of yellow legal paper. Other notes are more formal. I keep a file in my desk drawer of all the feedback I receive on my writing. I share notes, rejections, comments, and ideas because I want students to understand that their words, ideas, and stories should be unique and original but that all good writers learn from other writers and readers. Writers do not completely reinvent the wheel each time they sit down at a table or desk to write. Instead, they often have a collection of strategies, ideas, and examples to help guide their work.

Eric, a young man with a mild form of autism, raised his hand. He shared his story: "What I wrote about happened yesterday when I was in math class. A boy in the front row kept asking me why I am so ugly. He said it over and over again really loud. I know I look different than everyone else, but why didn't the teacher do anything about it? The teacher just stood there smiling. He heard what was happening and didn't do anything to help me." The class sat quietly listening as Eric told this story. Eric rarely spoke in class prior to this and his courage to share was powerful. Emma shook her head in disbelief and responded by saying, "This is not OK. This shouldn't happen to you, Eric, or to anybody." She stood up from her desk and moved to sit beside Eric. Interactions like these make me see what is possible in a learning environment. Even at the uncomfortable and young age of fourteen, students like Eric and Emma can take risks and support one another through sharing and truly listening to one another's stories.

As I heard pieces of these stories, I knew how important it would be to provide students with an audience for their powerful tales. As students listened to one another in respectful and careful ways, trust in our community grew. I was determined to find a way to share these stories with an audience outside our classroom walls.

Finding an Audience

> You look a long time till you find the right ears. Till then, there are birds and lamps to be spoken to, a patient cloth rubbing shine in circles, and the slow, gradually growing possibility that when you find such ears, they already know. (Nye 1995, 151)

I meet my friend, Harriet, at a bakery every Saturday morning to drink coffee and catch up on the week's news. Harriet is a fifth-grade teacher at a private elementary school across the river in southwest Portland. We share our stories, frustrations, resources, and ideas about teaching with one another as a supportive ritual. One Saturday early in the year, I told Harriet about the writing that took place that week in my ninth-grade classes and how the work was inspired by children's stories. I wanted students to revise and polish their stories to share with a real audience. Harriet was exhilarated about the project. She immediately suggested that my students write their stories as a collection and share them with her fifth-grade class.

These kinds of spontaneous conversations and ideas often move my teaching forward. I used to imagine myself as one of those teachers who had every lesson, every unit, and every year completely planned and prepared in September. Over time, I realized that it is essential to have clear ideas and goals for my students in the kinds of literacy skills I want them to leave with in June. However, the path to obtaining these skills can change and improve with every year. Oftentimes I've discovered that the most creative and successful curriculum ideas come about in surprising and unexpected ways. Many of my teaching and writing ideas come to mind randomly while I am hiking, gardening, cooking, doing yoga, and visiting with friends. During my first year teaching, a wise veteran teacher told me, "Jessie, remember that good teachers have good lives." Over the years, this advice has rung true time and time again. Another piece of advice that has served me well in my work came from Bill Bigelow in an article he wrote for *Rethinking Schools*: "Don't be a Lone Ranger. Teaching can be isolating if you let it. Establish a support group, a study group, a critical friends group, an action group—whatever you want to call it. Just because you may be in a classroom all alone with your students doesn't mean that you should reproduce that isolation outside the classroom" (2002, 13). Weekly meetings with Harriet became one of the ways I gathered inspiration and support for my teaching and kept myself from feeling isolated. Through one such conversation over coffee on a rainy Saturday morning, Harriet and I agreed to collaborate on this writing project. We decided to have our classes work together to revise and publish the stories of injustice.

The following Monday, I told my ninth graders that we were going to rework our stories to create a published collection for Harriet's fifth-grade class. Jordan's hand immediately shot up: "What do you mean? My story isn't going to work for that age. It's not really appropriate. It's too violent." Jordan's story was about a fight that took place on the basketball court and he was concerned that it was too graphic to share with younger students. We began a conversation about the ways in which our stories would need to be revised to fit the new goal and audience. I created guidelines and standards for their stories to help students have a clear direction for their writing and revision work (see Handout 1.3).

As students began to work on this essay, Harriet told her class about the project. Her fifth graders considered the books they had shared all year as read-arounds, literature sets, and independent reading choices shared in book reviews. Harriet's students brainstormed lists of what made those stories engaging to them. Then Harriet asked her students to write letters to my ninth graders about the elements of an engaging story based on their own experiences as readers and writers.

Stories of Injustice

Directions: In this assignment you will work to write, revise, and polish a narrative essay about a time in your life when you witnessed, participated in, or experienced an act of injustice. Here are some ways that you can approach this topic:

1. Write about a time when you were the object of discrimination or injustice.

2. Write about a time when you witnessed an act of discrimination or injustice.

3. Write about a time when you were involved in treating someone else unjustly.

4. Write about a time when you were an ally to someone who was the object of injustice.

Audience: Fifth-grade students, your peers, and your teacher.

Purpose: To share life experience with others in order to inform and teach about issues of justice.

Your paper must include the following:
1. an introduction
2. dialogue
3. setting description
4. character description
5. resolution (if there was one) and what you learned from this experience
6. conclusion—this can be a reflection looking back at this event with fresh eyes

Due Date: _____

In his letter, Josh wrote:

Dear Miss Singer's Students,

My connections tell me you are writing a children's book. I being a child, have read many children's books. Harriet also informs me that you're in need of guidelines to be of help. Here are several ideas you may use: A book must imprint a feeling in the reader of the book. Also, things can't end "happily ever after." Books must have a problem and not a common, "We're not best friends anymore" problem.

To keep a reader interested, you have to use ideas and issues that concern/interest kids (not a baby goat). Children also enjoy books that are humorous and funny.

I hope my suggestions are useful.

Alias: Jack Davidson

P.S. A good conclusion is always good too.

In her letter, Sandra included a list of ideas:

1. Include interesting characters or creatures.
3. Have exciting parts.
4. Describe in detail how the character looks, acts, or feels.
5. Try to make the book interesting.
6. Don't make everything all nice and joyful, because that is boring.
7. Make a problem in the story.

Hallie had the following suggestions:

First, you must have a catchy title to make the reader want to read the book. In the book, you must make relations to kids so that they are more entertained. In the end, you should not have everything be perfect, because then it makes your story boring. Instead, maybe you should leave a mystery or hook at the end for the reader to wonder about. You should have a moral or lesson so that the reader can put it back on the shelf as a changed person.

I shared these suggestions and letters with my ninth graders and the writing project's purpose changed immediately. Students thoroughly enjoyed the honest, animated feedback from their younger audience and the assignment became less about having to write an essay for English class and more about creating stories that would teach, inspire, and entertain younger writers and readers. I asked students to share their reactions to the project in a written reflection at the end of the class. Written reflections are quick and rough writing opportunities for students to check in with me regarding their progress and thinking surrounding a project. I often pass out yellow sticky notes or three-by-five-inch cards to my students in the last minutes of class and ask them to tell me what they learned that day, what they are thinking about the project, and what they need to do next to move their work forward. These reflections are a way for me to check in with students about their progress, questions, suggestions, and interests. I make it clear that these reflections are not graded but that they are a crucial part of class participation and help me to plan and prepare based on their needs. I also explain how metacognition, or thinking about your own thinking, is an essential skill in becoming a writer. My goal is not only that students will successfully write narrative, persuasive, imaginative, and expository pieces in my class, but that they will have skills and language with which to understand and articulate their own writing process. The more students understand their own process, the more control they have as writers.

Written reflections provide opportunities for students to put words to their learning and thinking. Margo wrote, "I am excited about this project. Although, as I am sure you noticed, I am not the biggest fan of editing. Overall, the experience will be well worth the trouble. I think this will turn out to be fun for us and the kids." Amanda wrote, "I think that by teaching these kids about things like this, real life problems, we are helping them to grow, learn, and accept that everyone and the world isn't perfect but that the world needs work." Jordan shared, "I can't wait to see how all the kids react and edit our stories!" Pete was less enthusiastic—"My honest thoughts about this project are that it's gonna be a drag. But, I will try to make it work as best as possible. Can't guarantee though. Let's see what happens." Sam had a specific concern since "my piece is about discrimination against teenagers. I don't know how to make it for a younger audience because people don't discriminate against ten-year-olds." These brief notes provided helpful insight into student reactions and questions about this writing project.

Revision

As a class, we chose a format and layout for our story collection. We decided to model our collection after the book *Tikvah*, which was one of the books I included in the initial children's book reading workshop. This wonderful text is a collection of essays and illustrations about human rights created by distinguished authors of children's books. *Tikvah* includes a written reflection and an illustration from each contributor. For example, one page is a story titled "The Brickyard," written by Marianna Mayer, which describes the horror of child labor and ways to get involved to work toward improving this dark reality. The opposite page is an illustration by Mayer that shows two girls carrying bricks on their backs, representing the brickyards of Nepal where young children are forced to work. Our class decided to allot two pages to each writer, just like in *Tikvah*; one page would be the story of injustice and the other page would be an illustration. We discussed how children's stories often need to be short in order to keep the reader's attention. I was not strict with students about a page limit, but I recommended that they cut the story down to five hundred words. After we decided upon this format, it was clear that we needed to revise our stories. I emphasized how editing writing is a skill that all writers need to know in order to match their writing to specific tasks, publications, and audiences. Margo was frustrated: "Ms. Singer, why do I have to cut my story up? I know it is still rough, but I like it. If I take out any details it won't be very good." Margo had a point. Although we wanted to keep our collection uniform and follow the advice of the fifth graders, we needed to find ways to keep the important details intact while dropping excess information. Students had to practice letting go of superfluous words in order to fulfill the goals of the project. I designed a writing workshop, "Cutting and Pasting," to offer an opportunity for students to practice editing.

I copied stories from Andrea Pinkney's *Let It Shine: Stories of Black Women Freedom Fighters* (2000) and asked students to work in pairs to find pieces from these stories that could be cut without losing the main messages. This editing workshop required students to read the stories, understand the main themes and messages, and then choose sections to edit out. This assignment was not completely fair because I gave students already edited and published pieces. It would have been more realistic to use stories that were still rough and clearly in need of editing, rather than already published works; however, students rose to the challenge. After reading and marking up the copies of their texts, students wrote reflections about what they noticed in the process of trying to edit writing. Hanna wrote, "I thought it was hard to pick sections to cut. The whole thing is really good. This made me have to really look at what was important to the story and what would be OK to leave out." Brandon wrote the following about his work as an editor: "What I noticed as an editor is that it's impossible to cut out sections and leave it at that. You need to add new connections and rearrange the piece so it can flow. If you just say, 'keep six paragraphs,' you can't take six existing paragraphs and expect it to work. It needs to be connected so it doesn't seem chopped up and confusing." Brandon's insight helped set him up to think about ways of editing his own piece to provide clear and smooth transitions. Sarah realized the difference between editing another writer's work and editing her own: "It's easier to cut someone else's work because you are not as attached to the words. It will be hard for me to find out what I'm going to cut from my paper because I love a lot of the details. The challenge will be to figure out how to make it flow together and not jump too far ahead."

After editing other writers' words, we began the process of editing and revising our own stories. I provided an editing questionnaire to help students think about their main idea, the tone of the piece, and sections they wanted to cut or revisit (see Handout 1.4).

As students revised their stories of injustice, I provided multiple examples of writing from writers who use editing and revision to improve their work. I invited one of my seniors, Anna, to share her process revising and editing a college admission essay. She talked about the choices she made when cutting it down to one page instead of five pages and the ways she rearranged and rewrote the essay to make it clear and effective. I also shared my own writing and revision process. Students worked together in peer review to offer helpful hints and suggestions. Peer review takes place when students share writing with their peers to receive feedback about successful aspects of the piece and ways to revise.

Peer review is often worthless unless writers have a clear sense of what to do to help their partners. I used hints that I acquired

Revision Questions

1. What do you hope the reader will learn from your story? What is one main point you hope he or she will walk away with?

2. Highlight the essential information and details connected to the main point and tone.

3. Read the remaining writing. Are there gaps in your story? Do you need to replace any of your writing? Do you need to add connecting phrases or words?

4. Go for it! Revise . . .

Due Date: _____

from Peter Elbow's *Sharing and Responding* (1989) to teach a quick lesson on peer review strategies to help writers ask their readers for what they need in feedback groups (see Handout 1.5).

The times I have placed students in writing groups without guidance they often become judges of one another's writing rather than helpful assistants. Elbow's guide gives students a way of helping one another that is not evaluative or judgmental. This kind of peer review is not about meeting specific criteria—instead, it is about response. The guidelines help the reader pay attention to his or her reading so that they may offer helpful feedback to the writer. This structure allows the writer to lead the feedback session with their own questions so that it remains safe and productive.

Writing Skills: Dialogue and Setting

As students began to revisit their stories of injustice, I wanted them to incorporate new writing skills into their narratives. I often teach skill lessons (Atwell 1998) in the first eight to ten minutes of class to inform students of specific writing and reading strategies. These lessons range from simple conventions, such as commas and quotations, to rhetorical strategies, like beginning with a powerful lead. I take the beginning of class to teach specific writing skills and strategies. I often use the beginning ten minutes of class or an entire week to allow students to practice a new skill in a variety of ways. Direct skill instruction, embedded in the curriculum at relevant and appropriate times, provides students with the necessary tools to improve as writers and readers. I have found that it is important that the skills are not introduced in random and disconnected ways. I choose specific skills to match where we are in the curriculum.

The essayists I admire most—Melissa Madenski, Joanne Mulcahy, David James Duncan, and John McPhee—all do a remarkable job of capturing the conversations they overhear or imagine. I want my students to understand the power of dialogue in their writing, and I hope to teach them some of the basic rules to do this successfully. One of my favorite teachers and mentors, Kim Stafford, writes about the power of dialogue to inspire writing: "By listening to the glories of conversation around me, I am moved to write, and I am reminded to listen closely to my own most quiet thoughts and dreams. In their inventive talk, my wise neighbors give me permis-

Peer Review Guide

Sayback

Ask readers: "Say back to me in your own words what you hear me saying in my writing. But say it more as a question than as an answer—to invite me to figure out better what I really want to say."

Pointing

Ask readers: "Which words or phrases stick in your mind? Which passages or features did you like best? Don't explain why."

Center of Gravity

Ask readers: "What do you sense as the source of energy, the focal point, the seedbed, the generative center for this piece?" (The center of gravity may not be the main point but rather some image, phrase, quotation, detail, or example.)

What's Almost Said or Implied

Ask readers: "What's almost said, implied, hovering around the edges? What would you like to hear more about?"

sion to take seriously my own internal voice" (2003, 17). The following is an example of the skill lessons I prepare to help my students succeed in their work incorporating dialogue into their narratives.

A Lesson on Dialogue

In *Bird by Bird* (1994), Anne Lamott describes the importance of good dialogue in writing: "Good dialogue is such a pleasure to come across while reading, a complete change of pace from description and exposition and all that writing. Suddenly people are talking, and we find ourselves clipping along. And we have all the pleasures of voyeurism because the characters don't know we are listening" (64). To introduce the significance of good dialogue, I gather selections from stories, essays, interviews, and news clips to share with my students. I use examples of dialogue from memoirs such as *Don't Let's Go to the Dogs Tonight: An African Childhood* (2003) by Alexandra Fuller and *A Heartbreaking Work of Staggering Genius* (2000) by Dave Eggers. I share interviews like one of Nelson Mandela from *O: The Oprah Magazine* and a recorded interview of a writer from the National Public Radio program *Fresh Air*. I ask students to remember a conversation from that morning or the day before and practice capturing it in as much detail as possible on the page. After students are exposed to multiple examples of dialogue and they have practiced writing dialogue on their own, I then take the time to share some of the basic rules of punctuation and grammar when writing dialogue (see Handout 1.6).

Students practiced using these rules to embed dialogue into their stories of injustice. Sam described how he was denied service at a Dunkin' Donuts because he is a teenager. He used dialogue to enhance his narrative:

> It was a clear and cold day. The temperature seemed to be about 30 degrees. If there had been clouds, it probably could have snowed. My friends and I made our way across the street quickly so we wouldn't hold up traffic and then we filed into the warm Dunkin' Donuts.
> "YOU NEED TO LEAVE!" I heard a voice yell. I looked up not knowing where the voice was coming from. I saw a lady behind the counter with an angry look on her face and her finger pointed right at us. "Are you buying anything?" the lady asked irritably.

Some Rules for Writing Dialogue

- Dialogue is enclosed in quotation marks. One set of quotations mark the beginning of the dialogue and the other set marks the end.

- A comma separates the actual quotation from the "he said," "she said," etc. Matt saw Jessie as she entered the kitchen.
  He said, "Hi, Jessie, it's nice to see you again."

- The comma and the period at the end of a quote come before the quotation marks.

- The first word of a quotation is capitalized because it is the beginning of a sentence . . . unless you are continuing a sentence.
  "Termination dust is what we call the first snowfall," Matt explained.
  "I can't believe it," she said, "it's been two years since I've seen Kenny."

- When a quotation ends with a question mark or an exclamation point, do not use a comma. These punctuation marks serve instead of commas.
  "Sit down!" he ordered.
  "Is it you?" she asked.

- When you are quoting or writing a conversation, be sure to start a new paragraph for each speaker.
  "Have you ever heard this band before?" my friend asked.
  "Never," I replied.

- When a person is repeating something that someone else said, use single quotation marks within the quote.
  "He said 'I need to be alone right now.' That's exactly what he said."

Emma used dialogue to start her story with flare:

> "Four hours of outside work?" whined the entire fourth-period class.
>
> "She's got to be kidding!" I said, shocked. "There's no way I'm going to do that!"
>
> It was the beginning of the fourth quarter of eighth grade and, as usual, no one had started the four hours of community service required to pass the class. I began brainstorming ideas in my head of how I could possibly receive an 'A' on my report card.

After each minilesson, I gave students time to practice new strategies in their own writing and then write a quick reflection about what was happening. In one of these reflections Danika wrote, "I feel like I need to shorten my story a lot. This may mean taking out details or focusing on only one aspect of what happened. My idea for the illustration is probably a picture of different scenes sort of intertwined. Currently, my main concern is cutting down my story and changing some of the word choices to fit the younger audience." The reflection writing helped students define their own needs and learning and helped me assess students' progress.

As we practiced new skills, revised, and shared our stories, I wanted students to move beyond merely telling about a difficult experience and into an understanding of how acts of injustice can lead toward significant learning and understanding. I emphasized how these stories were meant to be teaching stories to share with a younger audience and how they needed to do more than entertain. I wanted students to understand ways in which acts of wrongdoing or injustice can help to influence thinking and future action. Through hard work, practice, skill development, and revision, students created powerful stories. Leigh wrote her story about her experience as an athletic girl in physical education class.

There's a Sale at the Mall

"Come on girls, run! There's a big sale at the mall and you have to get there before it's over!" barked the P.E. teacher. It was a typical day in my freshmen physical education class and we were running a few laps around the school. But that day we had an awful "drill sergeant" substitute teacher who was so strict he seemed like he had come straight from the Marines. He was like a giant, complete with a blue jogging suit, a whistle, gigantic muscles, and a buzz-cut.

"Let's go! Run! I'm not kidding, ladies!" he screamed. Mary, Jenni, and I rolled our eyes and broke into a light jog. Contrary to the drill sergeant's intent, his earlier comment about the mall had not inspired us to run. The drill sergeant sprinted off, ready to torment other students. "A sale at the mall . . . like, I like totally can't wait you guys. Omigod!" chirped Jenni in a sarcastic tone. We laughed at how the drill sergeant did not understand teenage girls. We made a conscious effort not to run.

Discrimination is something that happens a lot in P.E. class. Girls are usually considered less athletic and weak compared to boys. But, when you think about it, fourteen-year-old boys tend to be a little on the scrawny side.

"I'm counting to five, everyone better be on this side of the weight room or it's twenty-five push-ups!" bellowed the substitute. Two weeks had passed since our last encounter with a substitute in P.E. and now we had to deal with Mr. S. Mr. S. is actually the athletic director at our school and he is a no-nonsense kind of man. "Today, we're going to do some arm exercises," he said. "I see a lot of skinny-armed girls in here, so ten pounds on each hand for the girls and twenty or twenty-five for the boys. But boys, if you don't think you can handle that much you can lift the GIRLS' weights." After those instructions, what boy would take less than twenty pounds? We did many repetitions of all sorts of strange lifts with our weights. My ten pounds in each hand was starting to feel like a ton. I cannot imagine what some of those little ninety-pound boys with twenty-pound weights in each hand felt.

Obviously, this type of discrimination against girls also affects boys. If a boy cannot handle as much as the rest, he is humiliated and forever teased. A lot of girls play sports and could physically handle much more than what P.E. teachers assign. For example, my friend Elizabeth plays soccer, tennis, and she runs and swims. During our P.E. fitness test, the boys do as many pull-ups as they can and the girls often just hang on the bar in the pull-up position. Elizabeth could do regular pull-ups, many more than some of the boys, if she was just given a chance.

The resolution to this unfair assessment of a student's physical abilities due to gender is just that P.E. teachers need to change some of their policies. Teachers should understand that a ninety-pound freshman boy will not be able to do more pull-ups than an athletically inclined freshman girl. Teachers should also know that not all girls are interested in running to a sale at the mall.

Ken used his story to share a lesson he learned about the power of language on the Internet.

Computer Words

The computer made a whirring noise and the lights flashed. It had begun my daily travel into the world of online games. I play computer games almost every day and had never run into any problems with, what I thought, was discrimination. I was never fazed by this or upset in any way until two weeks ago.

Two weeks ago, I was playing an online game called DoD (Day of Defeat). This is an online game about World War II and the Allies' assault on Germany. I was playing as an Allied officer. My team and I had come under fire from a machine gunner stationed across a bridge. As we secured the bridge leading into Anzio, an Axis squad of storm troopers started to move through a burning shop trying to reach our position. After a brief firefight, we dispatched the squad and moved onto the objective to secure our victory.

After we won, I leaned back and stretched in my chair. It had been a fun game, even if we totally annihilated the other team. As I glanced down into the left hand corner of my screen, I could see that the other team was not so happy about us winning. They started to use foul language and it steadily increased in volume. None of the insults affected me in any way at first. When people call me names online it normally has no meaning to me because how would someone halfway across the country know anything about me? That's what I thought until someone started to use the word "Jew" as an insult. I was shocked that someone would actually use "Jew" in a way to make me, I am part Jewish, seem bad or wrong in some way, especially, in a video game about World War II.

This was the first time that an insult online fazed me in any way. Someone using a term that relates to me made me take a long look at the words I use. It made me think of who I could be hurting with my language and attitude online. I have tried to change my ways while talking online and, I have to admit, it is hard. I think that everyone needs to think about how their actions will affect others around them.

Illustrations

As students worked individually and together to revise and edit their stories, I introduced an illustration workshop using the children's books we read at the beginning of the unit. I asked students to choose a few children's books to browse through and to carefully study the illustrations. I provided them with a set of questions to assist their study (see Handout 1.7).

Students began thinking about the kinds of images they could create to complement and tell their story. Matt wrote, "I want my illustration to be a pencil drawing or maybe paint. I suck at drawing people though. I'm not really sure, but I want it to convey a clear message." On the back of Matt's workshop questionnaire he created a rough sketch of his illustration. Amanda wrote that she wanted to create either a collage or a black-and-white painting. She planned to draw eyes to represent the women in her story who were always watching her. She wrote, "I want to create a sullen expression for the misunderstood and a kind smile for the lady by the door." Students created lists of the supplies they needed for their art and the times and places where they could get their work done. Veronica wrote, "I want to try a mixture of drawing and collage. I'm thinking of a picture of a small boy lying in the middle of the room crying with older kids laughing. I can start this Thursday in class, but if I don't finish it, then I will do it at my desk at home listening to music before I go to bed Friday night."

Setting clear and attainable goals helps set students up for success and is essential in teaching a diverse population. I try not to assume that all students know how to break projects down into realistic steps they can accomplish successfully. I do not assume that they all have access to art supplies or space at home to work. When I ask students what they need to successfully complete the project, I am better prepared to provide structure and support.

I find it helpful to invite other people to act as teachers or models for my students and to help teach specific skills that may not be my specialty. I invited one of my seniors, Allison, who is a serious artist and a wonderful writer, to help teach an illustration workshop to my ninth graders. Allison provided the prompt in Handout 1.8.

Illustration Workshop #1

1. Spend five to ten minutes browsing through children's picture books, focusing on the illustrations.

2. Which illustrations are you drawn to and why? (List at least two.)

Book title _____ Page _____

Because:

Book title _____ Page _____

Because:

3. What kind of illustration do you want to create for your children's story?

4. What image would connect with your piece? Explain.

5. What supplies do you need to create your illustration?

6. Where and when will you do the illustration? Be specific! (One day of class will also be reserved for this work.)

Requirements for your illustration:

1. It needs to fit on an 8½-by-11-inch page (a typical page of notebook paper).
2. You need to sign or initial and date your work (subtly, in a way that doesn't interfere with your artistic statement).

Due Date: _____

Illustration Workshop #2

Think back to your favorite books when you were a child. Can you remember the story or the characters' names? Can you remember the pictures? Now when we read books, the words create the images and paint the pictures in our minds. When we were children, these images were there on the page. Illustrations were elaborate and detailed or simple and plain, but they added dimensions to the story and fed our imaginations. Part of your assignment in writing your children's book is to create an illustration to connect to your story. You want to choose the most important or significant scenes in your piece to base your illustrations on. You won't be able to illustrate every sentence so choose a few that matter most. Freeze an image from that sentence or paragraph in your mind and then transfer it to paper. This is just a layout, you don't have to have any talent—the people can be stick figures. Once you have your layout, there are a few different ways to continue.

1. This method does require some skill, and it is probably the most obvious. Draw out your scene in more detail and color it with crayons, colored pencil, pen, etc. Your scene can be very realistic and detailed, very simple, or anywhere in between.

2. Your second option is collage. This method only requires that you operate a pair of scissors and a glue stick. You can create an entire picture by combining simple shapes like circles and squares of different colors. A very famous example is *The Very Hungry Caterpillar*, by Eric Carle.

Due Date: _____

Handout 1.8

Allison shared some of her own art and helped provide direct feedback and support throughout the workshop. I gave students time in class to begin their illustrations. Eric created a detailed and elaborate pencil drawing of the school's hallway. Diana created a collage with magazines and crayon drawings to show two girls chasing another girl up steep stairs (see Figure 1.1).

Figure 1.1: Diana's collage illustration for her children's story about bullies

Veronica drew an image of children taunting one another to go along with her story, "A Long Night of Taunting," about the negative effects of teasing (see Figure 1.2). In order to understand students' illustration choices and to push them to think about the ways in which art connected to their story, I ask students to answer the questions provided in Handout 1.9.

Emma wrote the following in response to the questions: "Making the illustration was the easiest part. The whole time I was writing the story, I had illustrations pictured in my mind. The

Figure 1.2: Veronica's drawing of children taunting one another

Illustration Reflections

1. Why did you choose your image(s)?

2. How does your illustration make a statement?

3. In what ways does your story tell what the illustration cannot?

4. In what ways does your illustration tell what your story cannot?

5. What else about this process do you want to share? (For example, what surprised you? What problems did you have to solve?)

Due Date: _____

illustration gave details that the words couldn't. The illustration also continued parts of the story I had to cut out." Sam described his desire to create something original. "I looked for a way to illustrate my story in a way that the other people in the class hadn't done yet, something different. I decided to show what the store in my story really looked like and this made the themes more clear. I changed my idea about what I wanted the illustration to look like a lot. I just tried different ideas until I found one I liked."

Writing Suggestions and Rewards

After students revised and polished their essays and completed their illustrations, I began compiling them to give to Harriet's fifth grade students for feedback. Before sending the stories to the fifth graders, each writer wrote a note asking advice for revision and offered suggestions for how to read the piece. Jennifer provided the following explanation and questions for her fifth-grade reader:

> When I first wrote my piece, it was five pages long and cutting it down to this length was a difficult process. I had to give up a lot of my favorite parts of the story. So, I am wondering if my story still makes sense? Is it clear and does it have a nice flow? Is this a good topic? Is it relevant to you as a fifth grader?

Ken worried that his story was not age-appropriate and focused his note to the fifth-grade editors on this concern. "I have never written a children's story before. I hope you guys can give me some hints. I don't exactly know what level books you are reading. Maybe some of my words are inappropriate for you? Let me know. I look forward to reading your comments."

Harriet's students provided wonderful suggestions and reinforcement. Harriet spends teaching time with her students throughout the year sharing effective strategies for responding to other writers' words. Her class acted as a safe and effective audience because they were also writers, editors, and readers. Many of the fifth graders asked my students important and helpful questions about the stories. In response to Matt's story about gang violence, Sabrina asked, "Did anything like this ever happen to you again? How old are you? Now, when you see people that look like that, do you make friends with them? Were you suspended?" The fifth-grade audience helped my students see important details they had left out and appreciated the hard work that went into the writing. Ben acknowledged Carson's hard work by writing, "I am drawn to how much you showed that kids aren't the only people who do bad things in your story. I also like your great and thorough descriptions of Frank, his store, and the entire incident. Do you think you will remember this incident for the rest of your life? When you hear the name 'Frank' in ten years, will your face still cringe with anger?"

The morning my students received the written feedback from the fifth-grade class, the room fell silent. My students sat quietly at their desks reading the words of advice, recommendations, and accolades from their fifth-grade reviewers. Matt looked up from his paper and said, "Ms. Singer, it would be so cool to meet these guys." Unfortunately, Harriet's class was on its way to outdoor school the following week and our schedules did not allow us to find a way to get our classes together. In the future, I will work to organize a meeting of the different groups to share stories.

Final Stories

These writing and reading workshops asked students to make a transition from thinking "hard stuff is just what we see and feel in our lives" to thinking "there are hurtful actions and behaviors that take place in our lives that we can stop or change for the better." Making this shift in thinking about day-to-day injustices took place in different degrees for each of my students. After receiving feedback from the fifth-grade class, my students had a few more days to polish and revise their pieces before the final deadline. Each student turned in the polished story to publish along with an illustration and a reflection letter. For the reflection letter, I asked students to respond to four questions about their stories:

1. What does your paper have to offer readers? What does it inform or teach?
2. Have you thought about the incident in this story often? Why or why not?

3. How does reading and writing stories about injustice help the cause of justice?
4. How does reading and writing about injustice lead you to think about social change?

Ken wrote about cruelty that occurred in middle school between different social cliques. He shared the following in his reflection letter: "I think the root of this cruelty is fear of something we don't understand, or maybe that we will become something that we make fun of. I think people often make fun of people because they're different. Once one person starts discriminating, then people join in just for the hell of it, as if it's a part of our nature. Slowly, our culture is getting more open-minded, which is the solution to all of this." Reading student reflection letters enabled me to see the kind of growth that took place through this project. Diana shared her wisdom in the following reflection:

> This paper has a variety of things to offer depending on the way you choose to read it. There is an interesting childhood event, typical and foolish, and the underlying message of how terrible it is to go along with the crowd and treat someone badly for no good reason. The ending doesn't really have a resolution for the event, but rather, introspection about how things might have happened differently. It is an explanation of something that all of us have done: teasing, and the idea that everyone may have their own personality, but that is no reason to ignore the respect they deserve.
>
> Tolerance is treating everyone with respect, not necessarily treating everyone the same. There are some things that are just not acceptable. Our society continues to struggle with this idea because of our past and the inner workings of society itself. As Americans, you find that the more power you have, the more respect you receive. People constantly strive to earn more recognition and respect by stepping on people and trying to prove their importance.

Diana's story described a class trip she went on in fifth grade where she and her friends ganged up on another girl because she seemed different than them. Toward the end of her story Diana describes what happened:

Rebecca was different. She didn't seem to be a shady character. My only explanation is that she was immature, but by running from her, creating a game to entertain ourselves, we were truly ignorant. Such behavior I cannot defend, I can only apologize and say that I have made sure to have more compassion and understanding for any other individuals who may produce the same feelings. This event has changed me because, though I try to have few regrets, every time I see Rebecca, at a school function or just around the neighborhood, I remember that night and I am ashamed of the way I treated her.

Students turned in their final stories and illustrations. I took the collection of stories and illustrations for copying and binding. I could not afford to create a copy for each student, so I created four copies for each of my ninth-grade classes and one for the fifth graders. When I brought the final "published" books to class, students huddled around the table to look at their final creation. My ninth graders created a thank-you card for the fifth graders and sent it along with their final copy of the story collection.

Extensions

There are a variety of ways to extend or enhance this writing project.

1. Plan a gathering to bring the two classes together to meet one another and share stories. Invite parents and friends.
2. Invite a children's author to speak to your class about writing and publishing stories.
3. Display stories and illustrations in school display cases.
4. Contact local publishers to ask for help with copies. Take your class to the publisher to learn about this process.
5. Organize a public reading of the stories at a local library, bookstore, or café.
6. Ask a coffee shop or café near your school to display the stories and illustrations as art on their walls.

Conclusion

Telling personal stories of injustice provides students with an opportunity to reflect on past experiences and consider ways in which they could have acted differently to create positive social change. These stories offer students a way to think about past experiences as learning lessons that may influence present actions in positive ways. This project provided structured lessons on writing a narrative essay including a lead, dialogue, setting description, character description, and a conclusion. Students used multiple texts to inform their writing, revision, and illustration. Collaboration with a younger fifth-grade audience provided helpful perspective and feedback for the project. Through skill lessons, peer review, and frequent reflective writing, students polished their work and kept-track of their own learning process. The stories of justice project provided a foundation for the whole unit on social activism because students began to think about the impact and influence of individuals to affect positive change. The next chapter shares how I use book choice to teach in-depth reading and to show examples of the life work of a wide range of activists.

References

Atwell, N. 1998. *In the Middle: New Understandings About Reading and Writing.* Second edition. Portsmouth, NH: Heinemann.

Bigelow, B. 2002. "Teaching to Make a Difference: Advice to New Teachers from Teachers Who've Been There." *Rethinking Schools* 17 (1): 134.

Demi. 2001. *Gandhi.* New York: Margaret McElderry.

Eggers, D. 2000. *A Heartbreaking Work of Staggering Genius.* New York: Simon & Schuster.

Elbow, P., and P. Belanoff. 1989. *Sharing and Responding.* New York: Random House.

Espada, M., ed. 2000. Foreword. *Poetry Like Bread: Poets of the Political Imagination.* Willimantic, CT: Curbstone Press.

Fuller, A. 2003. *Don't Let's Go to the Dogs Tonight: An African Childhood*. New York: Random House.

Giroux, H. 1987. "Critical Literacy and Student Experience: Donald Graves' Approach to Literacy." *Language Arts* 64 (2): 175–81.

Joosse, B. 2002. *Stars in the Darkness*. Illus. by G. Christie. San Francisco: Chronicle.

Lamott, A. 1994. *Bird by Bird: Some Instructions on Writing and Life*. New York: Pantheon.

Nye, N. S. 1995. *Words Under the Words*. Portland, OR: Eighth Mountain Press.

Pinkney, A. 2000. *Let It Shine: Stories of Black Women Freedom Fighters*. Illus. by S. Alcorn. San Diego: Harcourt.

Rappaport, D. 2001. *Martin's Big Words: The Life of Dr. Martin Luther King, Jr*. Illus. by B. Collier. New York: Hyperion.

Rockwell, A. 2000. *Only Passing Through: The Story of Sojourner Truth*. Illus. by R. G. Christie. New York: Alfred A. Knopf.

Skarmeta, A. 2000. *The Composition*. Illus. by A. Ruano. New York: Harcourt Brace Jovanovich.

Stafford, K. 2003. *The Muses Among Us: Eloquent Listening and Other Pleasures of the Writer's Craft*. Athens: University of Georgia Press.

Stevens, N. 1999. *Tikvah: Children's Book Creators Reflect on Human Rights*. New York: Sea Star.

Williams, T. T. 2004. "Terry Tempest Williams." In *Listening to the Land: Conversations About Nature, Culture, and Eros*, ed. Derrick Jensen. White River Junction, VT: Chelsea Green.

Winter, J. 2004. *The Librarian of Basra: A True Story from Iraq*. San Diego: Harcourt.

Book Choice

*We are what we do, especially what we
do to change what we are. . . . A literature born in the process of crisis and
change, and deeply immersed in the risks
and events of its time, can indeed help to
create the symbols of a new reality, and
perhaps—if talent and courage are not
lacking—throw light on the signs along
the road. To claim that literature on its
own is going to change reality would be
an act of madness or arrogance. It seems
to me no less foolish to deny that it can
aid in making this change.*

—Eduardo Galeano, *Poetry Like Bread*

Book Choice Philosophy

My mother and father read John Steinbeck's *Of Mice and Men*
(1938) in ninth grade along with Harper Lee's *To Kill a Mockingbird* (1960), George Orwell's *Animal Farm* (1945), and William
Shakespeare's *Romeo and Juliet* (2000). Twenty-five years later, I
read these books in my ninth-grade English classes. Now as a high
school English teacher, my department's book list for the ninth-
grade courses includes these exact titles. I believe in wonderful
classic books. Marvelous canonical texts allow students to enter
into fantastic worlds where ghosts haunt their troubled sons,
lawyers and families stand up against prejudice, animals speak,
and young couples fall into rebellious star-crossed love. Exposure
to classic texts also allows students to enter a wider conversation
in the world of academia. If I want to prepare all students for college, it is important to teach and provide awareness of "classic"
texts. If I want students to have the kind of cultural capital that

they will need to participate in an intellectual community of edu-
cated adults, then there is a body of shared texts that are cultural
possessions and mark you as a member. I tell students about parties I went to in college where people stood around talking about
their impressions of a scene in *Hamlet* and how I could not participate in the conversation because I had never read the play. My
students often laugh and say, "You must have gone to a really
nerdy college." They also hear me when I tell about a shared experience and language that comes with reading or recognizing certain books. I bring in newspaper articles, essays, and poems and
show students specific lines that cite famous works. I want students to understand that literacy allows them to open doors, not
only to the world of work, but to wonderful shared conversations
about classic characters and stories. I also try to teach these texts
in ways that invite students to think about issues of equity and
justice.

At the same time, we discuss the politics behind the term *classic*. I provide students with a list of often-taught classic texts and
we discuss the authors, cultures, and perspectives that are not represented by these texts. Sandra Lopez, an Oregonian book artist,
eloquently describes the role of teaching unfamiliar and diverse perspectives. "Once you've experienced one other way of seeing, you
begin to realize there are many different ways to describe the uni-
verse, many different ways to transmit knowledge. And then you
may begin to think about the fact that while our methods of trans-
mitting knowledge are very good, they can also exclude a great
many things, which could be of importance to us. Thinking about
this, you may begin to ask whether many of these things are will-
fully excluded, not on a level of individual but cultural will" (2004,
224). I ask students to think about how many of the "classics" leave
out people of color, poor people, people with disabilities, and
women. I believe in teaching classic works and realize that many
school districts mandate particular titles. Even so, I also want to
provide multiple opportunities for students to taste voices and perspectives that are not well represented by the canon. Like many
other teachers interested in progressive curricula and teaching, I
work to provide a balance in my reading curriculum between "classic literature" and diverse multicultural works.

For political and ideological reasons, I want the reading in my
classes to be consequential in the lives of my students. More

specifically, I want to see schooling and education further the cause of social justice. I am adopting the position that to understand literature is not simply to read it, but to identify with it in some way. We have a moral obligation as teachers to expose students to all kinds of people—disempowered, disabled, underprivileged, and privileged. With exposure to a diverse collection of human stories, students will inevitably read about injustice. A true critical literacy does not only understand these stories but takes action to make positive social change. Book choice helps extend opportunities in my curriculum to expose students to stories about people working for social justice. This chapter provides examples of reading workshop activities revolving around activism books of choice.

An emphasis on book choice is crucial in creating a balance between freedom and structure for students within a language arts curriculum. Students need a basic structure to serve as a foundation for their learning. A strong curriculum provides a launching pad to expand students' conversation about issues that matter in their lives and futures. In order to match the reading abilities and individual interests of a diverse student population, I provided a wide array of texts about activism for my students to read throughout this unit. Offering book choice alone is not sufficient in teaching literacy. Integrated within the use of book choice, I directly teach reading strategies. By teaching students to analyze, compare and contrast, and question diverse texts, they not only begin to understand how others think and write about activism, but also how activism touches their own lives. This reading unit provides students with important literacy skills for understanding difficult texts and multiple genres, and allows students freedom to choose books that connect to their interests regarding activism. Students had multiple opportunities to share their books and to learn about each other's choices within this literature unit.

Books of Choice on Activism

I discovered that my students were more engaged in learning when we stopped reading novels as ends in themselves and started reading and examining society—from cartoons to immi-

> gration laws to the politics of language—and taking action, as
> [James] Baldwin says, to "change it and to fight it." (Christensen
> 2000, vii)

I began in the fall to seek out resources to assist in forming a list
of autobiographies, biographies, and memoirs about people who
have worked to create positive social change. The list includes a
diverse and eclectic collection of writers and subjects. One of my
goals in collecting titles was to include a wide variety of books so
that the list would be accessible and compelling to all of my students. I intentionally included book titles that were available in
the school library, public library, and local bookstores. I also purchased multiple copies of some of the texts, which I assumed
would be particularly popular. I did not want lack of access to
books to exclude any student from participation or success in this
unit, and I wanted to find a range of books that ninth graders
would love. I created "Tips for Book Choice" and attached a book
list of "good reads" to help introduce my students to this reading
project (see Handouts 2.1 and 2.2).

"Tips for Book Choice" and the activism book list provided
clear expectations and guidance for students to select their own
texts. Working with a diverse classroom of readers, I have found
that providing this kind of support is invaluable. If I simply tell
them to "go find a book—any book—and read it," they often
flounder without support, structure, or purpose. When setting up
book choice, I make sure students have clear parameters surrounding their choices, support in finding texts, a realistic reading timeline, and clear expectations for the kind of work they will
complete in response to the text.

Popular Books

A few of the books I brought into class immediately grabbed students' attention, so I purchased multiple copies. *In My Hands*
(Opdyke 1999), an autobiography by a young woman who was a
Holocaust rescuer, was a popular choice with the young men and
women in the class. It is a poetically written first-person account
of a young girl who helped rescue Jews; I also loved it as an adult
reader. *Life in Prison* (Williams 1998) was a book that many students chose. This is a riveting story by a former gang member
whose work against gangs earned him a nomination for the Nobel

Tips for Book Choice

In the next unit, you have the freedom to choose one of your books! Since our focus is on the power of social action and making positive change, your book needs to be a biography, memoir, or autobiography of someone who has worked for positive social change. I've attached a booklist that will assist you in making a choice, but the list should not limit you. If you find a book that you believe is about a person who has worked for social change and it isn't on the list, it is probably fine; just check with me. Make sure the book topic interests you and the reading level is challenging but not overwhelming.

Places to find books:
*   Powell's Bookstore: www.powells.com
*   Laughing Horse Bookstore (local bookstore)
*   Public library
*   School library (possibly)
*   Parents, friends, teachers
*   Other local bookstores
*   Amazon.com

Due Date: _____

Handout 2.1

Bibliographies of People Changing the World: Good Reads for Adolescent Readers

Alexander, J. 2000. *Command Performance: An Actress in the Theatre of Politics.* New York: Public Affairs.

Armstrong, L. 2001. *It's Not About the Bike: My Journey Back to Life.* New York: Berkley.

Ashby, R., and D. Ohrn. 1995. *Herstory: Women Who Changed the World.* New York: Viking.

Ashwari, H. 1996. *This Side of Peace.* New York: Touchstone.

Azevedo, R. 2001. *Defending Andy: One Mother's Fight to Save Her Son from Cancer and the Insurance Industry.* New York: Life Issues.

Beals, M. 1994. *Warriors Don't Cry: A Searing Battle to Integrate Little Rock's Central High.* New York: Pocket Books.

Brown, C. 1990. *Septima Clark and the Civil Rights Movement: Ready from Within: A First Person Narrative.* Trenton, NJ: Africa World Press.

Buscher, S., and B. Ling. 1999. *Mairead Corrigan and Betty Williams: Making Peace in Northern Ireland.* New York: City University of New York Press.

Buss, F. L. 2001. *La Partera: Story of a Midwife.* Ann Arbor: University of Michigan Press.

Castaneda, J. G. 1998. *Companero: The Life and Death of Che Guevara.* New York: Vintage.

Century, D. 1994. *Toni Morrison: Author.* New York: Chelsea House.

Dalai Lama. 1990. *Freedom in Exile: The Autobiography of the Dalai Lama.* San Francisco: Harper.

———. 1997. *My Land, My People: The Original Autobiography of His Holiness, the Dalai Lama of Tibet.* New York: Warner.

Del Castello, R. G., and R. Garcia. 1995. *Cesar Chavez: A Triumph of Spirit.* Norman: University of Oklahoma Press.

Drucker, M. 1991. *Frida Kahlo: Torment and Triumph in Her Life and Art.* New York: Bantam.

Eagle, C. W. 2000. *Outside Agitator: Jon Daniels and the Civil Rights Movement in Alabama.* Tuscaloosa: University of Alabama Press.

Feldman, R. T. 2001. *Thurgood Marshall.* Minneapolis: Lerner.

Fradin, D., and J. Fradin. 2000. *Ida B. Wells: Mother of the Civil Rights Movement*. New York: Clarion.

Fry, V. 1968. *Assignment: Rescue*. New York: Scholastic.

Gandhi, M. 1960. *Gandhi's Autobiography: The Story of My Experiments with Truth*. Washington, DC: Washington Public Affairs Press.

Garcia, F. D. 2000. *Che: Images of a Revolutionary*. New York: Pluto.

Goodall, J. 2000. *Africa in My Blood: An Autobiography in Letters*. Boston: Houghton Mifflin.

Goodnough, D. 1996. *Jose Marti: Cuban Patriot and Poet*. Berkeley Heights, NJ: Enslow.

Gottfried, T. 2001. *Heroes of the Holocaust*. Brookfield, CT: Millbrook/Twenty-First Century.

Halasa, M. 1989. *Mary McLeod Bethune: Educator*. New York: Chelsea House.

Hatfield, M. 2001. *Against the Grain: Reflections of a Rebel Republican*. Ashland, OR: White Cloud Press.

Hildebrandt, Z. 2001. *Marina Silva: Defending Rainforest Communities in Brazil*. New York: City University of New York Press.

Hill, J. B. 2001. *The Legacy of Luna: The Story of a Tree, a Woman, and the Struggle to Save the Redwoods*. San Francisco: Harper.

———. 2002. *One Makes the Difference: Inspiring Actions to Save Our World*. San Francisco: Harper.

Hook, J. 2001. *Muhammad Ali: The Greatest*. Austin, TX: Raintree/Steck-Vaughn.

Hoose, P. 2001a. *It's Our World, Too! Stories of Young People Who Are Making a Difference*. Boston: Little Brown.

———. 2001b. *We Were There, Too! Young People in U.S. History*. New York: Farrar, Straus & Giroux.

Horton, M. 1998. *The Long Haul: An Autobiography of Myles Horton*. New York: Teachers College Press.

Kozol, J. 1991. *Savage Inequalities: Children in America's Schools*. New York: Harper Perennial.

Lawlor, L. 2001. *Helen Keller: Rebellious Spirit*. New York: Holiday House.

Ling, B. 1999. *Aung San Suu Kyi: Standing Up for Democracy in Burma*. New York: City University of New York Press.

Handout 2.2 (*continued*)

McCall, N. 1994. *Makes Me Wanna Holler: A Young Black Man in America*. New York: Random House.

McCall, T. 1977. *Tom McCall, Maverick: An Autobiography*. Portland, OR: Binford and Mort.

Michener, A. 1998. *Becoming Anna: The Autobiography of a Sixteen-Year-Old*. Chicago: University of Chicago Press.

Milio, N. 1970/2000. *9226 Kercheval: The Storefront That Did Not Burn*. Ann Arbor: University of Michigan Press.

Myers, W. D. 1993. *Malcolm X: By Any Means Necessary*. New York: Scholastic.

————. 2001. *The Greatest: Muhammad Ali*. New York: Scholastic.

Neal, S. 1977. *Tom McCall: Maverick*. Portland, OR: Thomas Binford.

Opdyke, I. 1999. *In My Hands: Memories of a Holocaust Rescuer*. New York: Anchor.

Parks, R. 1992. *Rosa Parks: My Story*. New York: Dial.

Partridge, E. 2002. *This Land Was Made for You and Me: The Life and Songs of Woodie Guthrie*. New York: Viking.

Pinkney, A. 2000. *Let It Shine: Stories of Black Women Freedom Fighters*. New York: Harcourt.

Reef, C. 2001. *A. Philip Randolph: Union Leader and Civil Rights Crusader*. Berkeley Heights, NJ: Enslow.

Remnick, D. 1998. *King of the World*. New York: Random House.

Rodriguez, L. J. 1993. *Always Running: La Vida Loca: Gang Days in L.A.* New York: Simon & Schuster.

Silverston, M. 2001. *Winona LaDuke: Restoring Land and Culture in Native America*. New York: City University of New York Press.

Sinnott, S. 1999. *Lorraine Hansberry: Award-Winning Playwright and Civil Rights Activist*. Berkeley, CA: Conari.

Steinem, G. 1995. *Outrageous Acts and Everyday Rebellions*. 2d ed. New York: Henry Holt.

Sterling, D. 1999. *Lucretia Mott*. New York: City University of New York Press.

Swain, G. 2001. *President of the Underground Railroad: A Story About Levi Coffin*. Minneapolis: Lerner.

Handout 2.2 (*continued*)

Thomas, P. 1974. *Down These Mean Streets: The Unforgettable Autobiography of an American of Puerto Rican Descent.* New York: Random House.

Tijerina, R. L. 2000. *They Called Me "King Tiger": My Struggle for the Land and Our Rights.* Houston, TX: Arte Público.

Weidt, M. 2001. *Voice of Freedom: A Story About Frederick Douglass.* Minneapolis: Lerner.

Williams, G. H. 1995. *Life on the Color Line: The True Story of a White Boy Who Discovered He Was Black.* New York: Penguin/Plume.

Williams, S. 1998. *Life in Prison.* New York: Sea Star.

Handout 2.2 (*continued*)

Prize. *Life in Prison* is also an appropriate choice for some of the struggling readers. People who had been in gangs and turned their life around were a popular subject, and *Always Running: La Vida Loca* (Rodriguez 1993) was another title that was often chosen for this reason.

I learned of new titles that students recommended. A biography of Muhammad Ali, *King of the World* (Remnick 1998), spread quickly through the classes, as some students were spurred on to read more than one book when they talked about their choices with friends. One student wrote the following in one of her reflections: "Matt says *King of the World* is the best book he's read since *The Cat in the Hat* [Seuss 1957]. I'm going to read it next!" Student responses to book choice were overwhelmingly positive. In one of her reflections, Jenna highlighted a key finding: "What's working for me in this unit is the fact that I got to choose my own book because it's something I want to read. It's kind of weird, though, because I enjoyed *Kaffir Boy* [Mathabane 1995] when we read it as a whole class. Yet there is something different about choosing your own book."

There are definitely times when I want to expose students to books they would not otherwise find on their own, such as *Kaffir Boy*, which I teach as a shared class novel during the South Africa unit early in the year. Often unfamiliar and seemingly distant texts make way for important, challenging, and unexpected learning. Students will lead teachers to books and areas of interests that we often would not find on our own. I discovered early in the unit how important book choice is in engaging students' interest, involvement, and commitment to the work. As Danika wrote: "The key part of this entire unit has been the book we chose. I am thrilled with my book choice. It is one of those small miracles that I happened to pick out of hundreds of options, and I find it fascinating. Because I love my book, I can easily write detailed pieces about one part or another."

Though there are always class favorites, it was also crucial that individual choices outside of the provided book list were honored. Danika read *Where Rag Dolls Hide Their Faces: A Story of Troubled Children* (Koplow 1990); this book about a child psychotherapist was new to everyone in the class. Margo chose *This Side of Peace* (Ashwari 1996), a challenging autobiography of Hanan Ashwari that I found fascinating but quite difficult in parts. I would not have guessed that this dense text would resonate with Margo. Paul made an equally surprising choice: the biography of Jose Marti— the Cuban patriot, poet, and activist. This was a dry and complicated text. Paul often struggled with his reading; however, as a Latino poet himself, he was drawn to learn more about this intriguing man who shared his love for words. The list below shows the range of choices the students made with their books.

Period 1

Student Name	Book Title
Jenni	*In My Hands*
Matt	*Gandhi's Autobiography*
Margo	*This Side of Peace*
Jordan	*Makes Me Wanna Holler*
Emma	*In My Hands*
Lisa	*In My Hands*
Danika	*Where Rag Dolls Hide Their Faces*
Corinne	*In My Hands*
Diana	*Defending Andy*
Sam	*In My Hands*
Jose	*Becoming Anna*
Justin	*Always Running*
Erik	*Rosa Parks: My Story*
Kenzo	*Helen Keller*
Ken	*Makes Me Wanna Holler*

Chelsea	*Always Running*
Veronica	*Always Running*
Nate	*Life in Prison*
Spencer	*Jose Marti*

Period 2

Student Name	Book Title
Carson	*In My Hands*
Taylor	*King of the World*
Erin	*Africa in My Blood*
Coco	*Freedom in Exile*
Jeremy	*Freedom in Exile*
Sarah	*Makes Me Wanna Holler*
Sean	*Tom McCall: Maverick*
Leigh	*Savage Inequalities*
Mary	*Warriors Don't Cry*
Lisa	*I Know Why the Caged Bird Sings*
Justin	*Legacy of Luna*
Michelle	*Outrageous Acts and Everyday Rebellions*
Jennifer	*Outrageous Acts and Everyday Rebellions*
Eric	*King of the World*
Joe	*Life in Prison*
Rachel	*Down These Mean Streets*
Brandon	*Malcolm X*
James	*King of the World*
Paul	*Cesar Chavez: A Triumph of Spirit*
Chelsea	*It's Our World, Too!*
Danny	*Malcolm X*
Ben	*Malcolm X*

A Good Fit

> Books can make a difference in dispelling prejudice and build-
> ing community: not with role models and literal recipes, not
> with noble messages about the human family, but with
> enthralling stories that make us imagine the lives of others.
> (Rochman 1993, 19)

"Look at the book I found Ms. Singer! It was on a shelf in the living room and my mom suggested that I read it for this class." Margo smiled as she showed me her book, *This Side of Peace*, and then sat down to compare her selection with other students. The day students arrived with their activism texts I arranged the room in a circle and asked them to share the titles of their books, what they knew about the book, and how they found it. Sharing about the books established a group investment in the reading project and helped to reveal the many ways to find good books. I am always impressed by the variety of books students find with the help of parents, friends, librarians, and teachers. Students are often thrilled to have the opportunity to choose their own books to read. With that said, there are always a few students who arrive in class without books, which is disappointing. I asked these individuals to choose from the books I kept in the classroom for the unit. Whenever I provided choices for students within the curriculum, I made sure that there was a support plan in case they did not come to class prepared. Rather than spending my time frustrated at students for forgetting books at home (which is a human mistake) or not having easy access to academic materials, I make sure there are ways to assist these students so that they may always participate. I have found that this kind of scaffolding helps to foster a safe learning community where students are not separated, left out, or punished for making mistakes or coming from less privilege than their peers.

The first day students arrived with their books I stressed that they could always change their minds about what book to read, but that it was important to do so before becoming too invested in the class projects. I said something like, "If you start reading your book and realize that it does not capture your attention and it is not a good fit, then find another. I am willing to help you find a book that feels worth reading." Reminding students that decisions about the kinds of books they want to read is a process that all strong readers go through helps them to begin to think about the kinds of texts that pique their interests. I explain how I often start a book and then realize a few chapters into it that the story is dry or that another book on my shelf better fits my mood. Still there are some readers who choose to finish any text they start. Often, when reading books of choice this kind of "stick-to-itness" is more an exception than the rule.

I remind students that there are different kinds of books and different reasons for reading different kinds of texts. When we read a common text as a class, there is a shared experience revolving around the story, the characters, and the book's context and meaning. When participating in this kind of reading exercise, it is important to read the book even if it does not feel like a perfect fit because it is a "ticket" into the shared conversations and learning in the class. We talk about how this kind of reading is similar to and different from reading separate texts we choose. I want students to see the real-world value of both of these kinds of reading activities. We talk about the popularity of book groups outside of school settings—how people enjoy learning and conversing about shared texts. We also discuss the kinds of books readers choose on their own that they may or may not choose to share with others. Often English classes place more value on reading shared texts than on any other kind of reading experience. Students need to know how to read, question, reread, write, and talk about unfamiliar and challenging texts. These skills not only prepare students for the academy and the workplace, but for their lives as readers. Students may learn all of the above reading skills and share important learning experiences while reading books they have selected. The common activism theme, time to read and share in class, and reading workshop activities all worked to create a kind of glue that helped hold the class together while reading various books.

First Impressions

Within the first days students began reading their books, I found ways to check in with them about whether or not the books had caught their attention and fit their needs as readers. Struggling readers often find books that are too difficult or too long to get through in the allotted time. I try to encourage students to feel challenged by their texts, but not so challenged that the pages feel intimidating and boring. Nate, who was a struggling reader, started off reading Nathan McCall's *Makes Me Wanna Holler* (1994), about a gang member who makes dramatic changes in his life. This is a thick and challenging book that immediately overwhelmed Nate, so he quickly switched to a more accessible and wonderfully written book, *Life in Prison* (Williams 1998), which is also about a gang member. For fast readers, I suggested that they read more than one book so that they learn as much as possible about activism work and remain engaged with the curriculum. There is no competition or comparison in this kind of setup. Instead students know that my expectations are high and that it is more enjoyable to be challenged than bored. It is never an option in my class to do nothing at all; when students finished their books early, they rarely argued about picking up another related book. A wonderful side effect of book choice is that students begin to have confidence that they can find a good book and that they will actually enjoy reading it. This arrangement requires a shift in perspective about what it means to teach reading. Rather than testing to see if all of my students can read the same number of pages in the same amount of time and acquire the exact same knowledge, this setup allows for students to take the time they need to carefully read so that they may all succeed with the related writing, discussions, and projects. In a letter describing his progress, Jordan wrote the following about the impact of book choice on his learning: "The past month or so, I've felt like I have had no heart behind my work. I was just writing to get the job done. But when I started *Makes Me Wanna Holler*, the book really brought my heart back to my work. I can relate to what's happening to the main character in the book. I'm stoked to read on." Interviewing students about their books and asking them to write their first impressions helped them articulate the qualities of their books that were most important to them as readers. This information also helped me make sure students were reading books that were a good fit. In a quick-write, I asked students to share their first impressions of their books.

Quick-Write 2.1

Please take five minutes to write your first impressions of your book.

- What do you think of the story so far?
- What characters, events, and details stand out to you? Why?
- Does this book feel like a good fit for you? Explain.

In reading Ashwari's *This Side of Peace* (1996) (about the Arab-Israeli conflict in the Middle East), Margo wrote the following after reading the first couple of chapters: "The voice of the main character really has me hooked. I also love learning about this era and conflict. It's interesting to hear about it from a Palestinian's view; mostly all I hear out in the news is the Israeli perspective. I enjoy how the author gives you history about the happenings, but it doesn't seem boring or factual. I admire her father; he is strong-willed and devoted to his cause. I think I am going to stick with this book, so far, I like it!" Emma provided an enthusiastic reaction to Irene Opdyke's book *In My Hands* (1999):

> I'm very interested in Irene, the main character. She comes across as a person without grudges and prejudice. She seems happy and like she's waiting for her chance to make a difference. I really enjoy the attitude she has because she puts others before herself, which is no easy task. I'm also drawn to the description in the story. The author does a good job of setting the scene. The characters, home, and town are all described with amazing detail. I'm only on page 18, but I can already imagine Irene's childhood in peaceful Poland. I'll continue reading this book for sure because the story grabbed me right away. I like getting the background of the character first, and that's what the author has done. That way the story all pulls together in the end.

Instead of testing or quizzing students over their reading, I asked them to write their reactions to the books. This kind of written reflection served the same purpose as a quiz. I could see where students were in their reading and it gave me a sense of their impressions, comprehension, and questions. Through this kind of informal writing, I also learned how students connected their texts to the activism unit as a whole. Students like Michelle began to think about how people become involved in activism. She read Gloria Steinem's *Outrageous Acts and Everyday Rebellions* (1995) and wrote the following in her first impression quick-write: "I am really enjoying my book. It is a collection of essays written over the course of Steinem's time as an activist. What I like about the book is how Gloria tells why she felt the way she did about women's roles and the changes that she made to help women. People don't really realize how much one determined person can make happen, but this book has really shown me the power of an individual to make change."

Literary Timelines

As students read, I wanted them to begin to think about the kinds of life events the activists experienced that helped shape their work. I hoped students would see in each of their books how any kind of lifework happens over the course of a lifetime with support and practice. I assigned students to keep a time-line of the author's life events leading up to their activism work. My goal was that students clearly articulate the key life events of their chosen activist so that after reading the book they could successfully write an expository piece that I called an "activism article" about the person's lifework (see Chapter 3 for writing workshop). I provided simple and concrete instructions for this assignment (see Handout 2.3) as well as a model (see Figure 2.1).

The timeline assignment was an easy way for students to practice taking notes while they read. I taught students what it means to annotate texts with sticky notes, bookmarks, and a reading journal. I gave out little bookmarks that I call "meaning marks" with blank spaces to keep track of new words they come across as they read. Justin came up to me one morning when the class was quietly reading their books and asked, "Ms. Singer, I keep reading my book but I don't remember anything I read. I don't know what to do." I sat down with him and showed him how to keep a piece of paper next to his book as he reads, creat-ing an outline of each day's reading (see Handout 2.4). At first he resisted this idea—"That's gunna be a lot more work." I suggested that he just give the strategy a try and wait to decide whether it was worth his while based on if it worked well for him. With practice, Justin became an avid notetaker over the course of the year. He told me that this helped him keep track of what hap-pened as he read a book—otherwise the events and the charac-ters all seemed to jumble together. He also learned how to divide his reading up to make completing the whole book more man-ageable. He wrote me a note sharing his reading plan: "My book is great. I am going to stick with it even though it is hard to read and kinda long. If I use the methods we came up with in class, I think that I can finish it in time. I just need to read a chapter a day and then I'm pretty sure I can get it done." Reading work-shops that revealed simple, yet essential, reading strategies helped students make sense of their texts.

Activist Timeline

Create a timeline of the major events in your activist's life:

1. Choose six to eight key dates. You may fill these in as you progress in your book.

2. Include an explanation that describes each date.

At the top or bottom of the page, include a quote by the person that you feel shows who they are and what they believe in. If one quote is not enough to show this, feel free to use two!

Due Date: _____

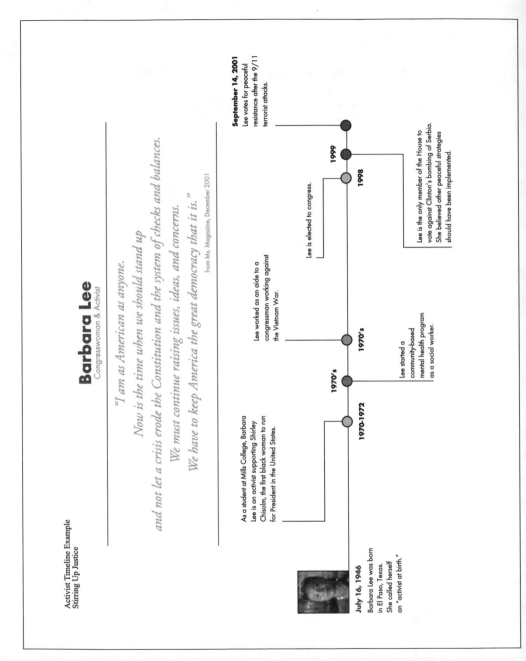

Activist Timeline Example
Stirring Up Justice

Barbara Lee
Congresswoman & Activist

"I am as American as anyone.

Now is the time when we should stand up

and not let a crisis erode the Constitution and the system of checks and balances.

We must continue raising issues, ideas, and concerns.

We have to keep America the great democracy that it is."

from Ms. Magazine, December 2001

September 14, 2001
Lee votes for peaceful resistance after the 9/11 terrorist attacks.

1999

1998

Lee is elected to congress.

Lee is the only member of the House to vote against Clinton's bombing of Serbia. She believed other peaceful strategies should have been implemented.

Lee worked as an aide to a congressman working against the Vietnam War.

1970's

1970's

Lee started a community-based mental health program as a social worker.

As a student at Mills College, Barbara Lee is an activist supporting Shirley Chisolm, the first black woman to run for President in the United States.

1970-1972

July 16, 1946
Barbara Lee was born in El Paso, Texas. She called herself an "activist at birth."

Figure 2.1: Example of an activist timeline for Congresswoman Barbara Lee

Time to Read

As students read their activism books, I wanted them to interact, react, and respond to these strong and inspirational stories. In order to do this, I knew I had to provide time in class to focus on reading. We read our books of choice silently for fifteen to twenty-five minute chunks of time three times a week. This time was precious. In order to establish the importance of reading, I have never found that it is enough to talk about books in class and to make all the reading homework. When students are provided with scheduled, purposeful, and quiet reading time in class, they have more of a chance to become connected to their books. My students are always required to read for homework, but this work begins and is reinforced in the classroom. During this time, I quietly read a book about an activist as well, and I scan the room collecting data about students. I notice if students are reading, whether they have come prepared with their books, and if they are about to finish their books and need new ones. I often write in my teaching journal during this time to take note of what is happening in the classroom and the unit as a whole. The following is an entry from May, written during a quiet reading time:

> What I keep thinking about is that even though we are all reading different books, this is such a shared experience. Students are talking about their books. Jennifer and Sam sit next to each other and when Jen found a good part in her book on Gloria Steinem, she halted Sam's reading and had him read a page of hers. Justin, who is often tired, often yawning, and often late in turning in work, has already read one book and is on to his second. Things are not magical as I always wish they would be. There are still students who did not show up with a book the first day and had to borrow from me or go to the library. But they are reading now, and Corinne, who came unprepared the first day, has now read two books on activists at the time of the Holocaust and she is beginning her third.

Reading Strategies

Each morning, before the room fell silent for reading time, I taught a reading strategy for students to practice while they

Reading Outline

1. Write a couple of sentences to summarize what was happening in the book the last time you read. (If you need to skim through the pages that you read last time, this is a great strategy for re-engaging your reading mind.)

2. Keep track of three main events or things that capture your attention as you read today. Jot them down below and explain why each event stood out to you.

   a.

   b.

   c.

3. As you finish your reading for today, briefly summarize what happened and why these events are important to the story as a whole.

Due at the end of class

Handout 2.4

read. These lessons included strategies such as creating a reading outline, responding to quotes that resonate, and annotating their text. I also gave students a writing or reading task to complete along with their reading for the day. These lessons gave students something to look for, react to, or analyze in their books. Having clear and manageable tasks to accomplish while reading gave students purpose, structure, and goals for the morning's reading time. I often asked a simple question, like the one that follows, to initiate students recording and reacting to their reading:

> What are some of the beginning signs in your book that the person is someone who will work toward positive change in his or her life? As you read, record three to four quotes that exemplify this move toward the work of an activist. After you record these quotes, write your reaction to each of them. Remember that your response can be in the form of a question, a gut reaction, a comment, or an idea that you want to remember.

In response to this prompt, Jennifer wrote the following about Gloria Steinem: "Gloria Steinem worked as a campaign leader for McGovern who was running for the presidency. She realized that even though she worked with him, that because she was a woman, her main job was to make coffee and do other chore-like things. Gloria Steinem used this experience as an inspiration to make change happen. She said, 'Women are never again going to be mindless coffee-makers in politics or unconfident reporters who fail to see our own half of the world. There is no such thing as a perfect leader. We have to learn to lead ourselves.'"

Book Hunt

> After reading about this wonderful activist, I see the world differently. This story makes me think of what I want to do that will create positive social change in the world. You have to follow your heart and let it take you to that special place of being a social activist. (Lisa, ninth grade)

I gave students three weeks to read their books of choice. The majority completed their books by the deadline and the few stu-

dents who needed a bit more time still participated in the culminating activities and final writing workshops revolving around
the books. After three weeks of reading workshops, strategy
lessons, and writing projects, I asked students to bring their
books to class for a book hunt. I brought in donuts and punch
for students to enjoy as they spent their time in class learning
and sharing about their books. I gave each student a "Stirring
Up Justice Book Hunt" handout (see Handout 2.5) and invited
everyone to mingle and talk about the books. This activity has
always been a wild success. Students thoroughly enjoyed teaching about the activists and learning about other kinds of lifework from the stories read by peers. We spent at least a half an
hour talking and sharing about our books before I asked everyone to sit down to write a reflection about the book hunt (see
Handout 2.6).

The book hunt reflection served as a way for me to assess what
students learned through sharing their books and it also allowed
me to introduce the culminating project for the whole activism
unit. I began to explain to students how they would be working
to create activism projects of their own.

Justin wrote the following in his reflection about the book
hunt:

> The book that caught my attention was *In My Hands*. Although
> I have read dozens of books about World War II and how peo-
> ple hid the Jews from the Nazis, this one seems the most excit-
> ing out of the ones I got to talk about today. This book also
> seemed more descriptive than some of the other books I've read
> about this topic. People did such a great job of discussing this
> book.
>
> I thought the book hunt was a great way to widen our hori-
> zons to other books and to think about other types of litera-
> ture than we are used to reading. What really helped me was
> to sit myself down in a big group of people and just listen.
> When someone was done, I shared about my book. This was a
> good way to not only learn about other books, but we got to
> learn about each other and what type of literature we like. I
> learned that people like to flock to one book. A lot of people
> read *In My Hands*.

Stirring Up Justice Book Hunt

1. Find someone whose book has a main character that makes an important change. What's the book? What's the change?

2. Find someone whose book deals with themes of racial justice. What is the book? What are the issues?

3. Find someone whose book deals with environmental issues. What is the book? What are the issues?

4. Find someone whose book honors working-class jobs or working-class life. What is the book? How is the work or working class honored?

5. Find someone whose book deals with a conventional topic in an unconventional way. What's the book? How does it deal with the topic?

6. Find someone whose book has incredibly strong women characters. What is the book? How do the women manifest their strength?

7. Find someone whose book deals with some aspect of imperialism or anti-imperialism—i.e., with foreign domination and resistance to domination. What is the book? What people or incidents are involved?

8. Find someone whose book is filled with hope. What is the book? What is it about the book that leaves readers hopeful?

Handout 2.5

Book Hunt Reflection

Please take the time to answer the following questions with thoughtfulness and detail.

1. From the books you learned about today, which book caught your attention and why?

2. What did you think of the book hunt? What worked for you and why? What did you learn today?

3. How did the book hunt inform you or give you ideas in creating and thinking about your final social activism project? Explain your thinking.

After reading through students' reflections, I began to see the impact of the activism books on their thinking about issues of equity and justice. Lisa wrote how hearing about Diana's books sparked her thinking about her own interest in working toward change to help underprivileged children: "This book hunt was helpful because it gave me a few options for what I can do for my own final project. I could work for social change by helping troubled children. I got this idea from Diana's great description of her book." Margo wrote the following reaction to the book hunt and how it moved her thinking about activism work forward:

> I liked the book hunt. I thought it was cool to learn about other people's books. I found all the activists to be amazing and determined people. I enjoy thinking about some of the same books in different ways. I learned that there are a million different dimensions and aspects to any book. When I kept explaining my book to people and hearing about other people's books, it made me want to do a project about discrimination. I have this idea, sort of a dream if you will. I want to paint a mural of tolerance on the school by the gym. There is a big blank brick wall there and I thought if I paid for the materials and organized the people to help, I could do it! The mural would show all different sorts of people together, tolerating each other and learning to love each other's differences. Perhaps at the bottom it would say something like "It is our differences that make us beautiful."

The work surrounding book choice and activism provided multiple opportunities to learn about and understand the work of activists. This reading unit allowed students to find a focus connected to their own interests. This reminded me of one of the things that inspires people toward action, change, and discovery, which is the feeling that out in the world there are voices that remind us of our own. Students began to learn about other people making choices that caught their attention and inspired their own thinking. The books of choice allowed students to dive into stories about faraway people. The stories made these people seem vibrant and real. Students learned how people like the Dalai Lama, Muhammad Ali, Julia Butterfly Hill, Nathan McCall, Gloria Steinem, and Tom McCall are all connected to families, schools, neighborhoods, trauma, and hope. These books gave students sophisticated and complex stories to practice honing their reading skills and to begin to think about activism in their own lives.

References

Ashwari, H. 1996. *This Side of Peace*. New York: Touchstone.

Christensen, L. 2000. *Reading, Writing, and Rising Up*. Milwaukee, WI: Rethinking Schools.

Espada, M., ed. 2000. Foreword. *Poetry Like Bread: Poets of the Political Imagination*. Willimantic, CT: Curbstone Press.

Koplow, L. 1990. *Where Rag Dolls Hide Their Faces: A Story of Troubled Children*. New York: Dutton.

Kroll, B. 1992. *Teaching Hearts and Minds: College Students Reflect on the Vietnam War in Literature*. Carbondale: Southern Illinois University Press.

Lee, H. 1960. *To Kill a Mockingbird*. Philadelphia: Lippincott.

Lopez, S. 2004. *In Listening to the Land: Conversations About Nature, Culture, and Eros*. White River Junction, VT: Chelsea Green.

Mathabane, M. 1995. *Kaffir Boy: The True Story of a Black Youth's Coming of Age in Apartheid South Africa*. New York: Random House.

McCall, N. 1994. *Makes Me Wanna Holler: A Young Black Man in America*. New York: Random House.

Opdyke, I. 1999. *In My Hands: Memories of a Holocaust Rescuer*. New York: Anchor.

Orwell, G. 1945. *Animal Farm*. London: Secker & Warburg.

Remnick, D. 1998. *King of the World*. New York: Random House.

Rochman, H. 1993. *Against Borders: Promoting Books for a Multicultural World*. Chicago: American Library Association.

Rodriguez, L. J. 1993. *Always Running: La Vida Loca: Gang Days in L.A.* New York: Simon & Schuster.

Seuss, Dr. [T. S. Geisel]. 1957. *The Cat in the Hat*. New York: Random House.

Shakespeare, W. 2000. *Romeo and Juliet,* ed. J. Levenson. New York: Oxford University Press.

Steinbeck, J. 1938. *Of Mice and Men*. New York: Triangle.

Steinem, G. 1995. *Outrageous Acts and Everyday Rebellions*. 2d ed. New York: Henry Holt.

Williams, S. 1998. *Life in Prison*. New York: Sea Star.

Writing into Activism

I suddenly realized . . . I command the
space to raise a dissenting voice, and if I
don't do it, it's as political an act as
doing it . . . to stay quiet is as political
an act as speaking out.

—*Arundhati Roy*

Turning Points

Arundhati Roy, author of *The God of Small Things* (1997) and the collection of political essays *Power Politics* (2001), explains in her documentary film *DAM/AGE* how her work as an activist began after the wild popularity of her first novel when she experienced a growing awareness of the disconnect between her success as a writer and the bleakness surrounding her in the political and environmental climate of her homeland, India.

> *The God of Small Things* became more and more successful and I watched as in the city I lived in the air became blacker, the cars became sleeker, the gates grew higher and the poor were being stuffed like lice into the crevices, and all the time my bank account burgeoned. I began to feel as though every feeling in *The God of Small Things* had been traded in for a silver coin, and if I wasn't careful I would become a little silver figurine with a cold, silver heart. (2002)

Roy began work on a bold and controversial campaign against the Narmada dam project in India, and she continues to use her gift as a writer to fight for issues of equity. Her decision to work as an activist was not spontaneous; rather, it grew along with her work and through powerful lived experience.

Mark Mathabane, author of *Kaffir Boy* (1995), visited my class in November 2002 after my students had read his autobiography. He talked about knowing from the time he was a young child living in the shantytowns outside of Johannesburg, South Africa, during apartheid that he wanted to find a way to work toward a better life. He described the first time he walked into a library and how he was filled with overwhelming joy and curiosity. His ability to read and write changed his life and helped him escape poverty. He gave his talk to our class in the school's library and shared how it saddened him that school libraries in the United States are often vacant and underfunded. He pointed to our school's library stacks and said, "There is freedom found within these books. I remember feeling freedom when I first walked into a library and that feeling has stayed with me and helped me escape poverty. I am now a writer and a teacher." His words deeply affected my students and revealed how difficult life experiences have the potential to instruct and alter people's paths in life. In a reflection about Mathabane's visit, Spencer wrote, "Mr. Mathabane is a real hero in my mind because he lived through apartheid, learned to read from scraps of newspaper and magazines and then escaped to a better life. The fact that he became a successful writer and wrote books about his childhood is nothing short of amazing." Mathabane modeled success as both a writer and as a person devoted to influencing progressive change in schools. Later in the year, I wrote in my teaching journal about the impact of Mathabane's visit on my students' thinking and how it served as a turning point in our time together:

> Looking back on this year with my freshmen, a turning point took place for them at the end of the South Africa unit when Mark Mathabane gave a talk. Having an author visit whose story they had read was powerful. I think it jumped students out of their own life lens completely. This is a reminder that no matter what I may plan or think will bridge students from their worldview to a broader one, what makes the outside— the new—the different—the "other" seem close and connected is often unexpected and is often the human story turned alive and real.

Roy and Mathabane both experienced turning points in their lives that helped shape their interests in activism. What we grow to care about often takes place over time and as a result of what we experience or witness. My dear friend Eve-Marie's passion for politics grew after moving to a conservative town in Idaho where her values, for the first time in her life, represented a minority opinion. She quickly began to find ways to use her art and her organizing skills to voice opinions that mattered to her deeply about women's rights and support for the arts. Thinking about how and why people are moved to act as agents of change helped me to imagine a writing task for my students. I asked them to write about an event in the life of the activist they were studying that could be considered a "turning point" in the activist's path toward activism. I used the term "turning point" to define a place or time in an individual's life where a passion or awareness is truly sparked.

This turning point writing workshop served as an important learning opportunity to help students understand how life goals and passions are often acquired through hardship and a deep sense of connection to a particular cause. In order to provide models for students of writing about turning points in other people's lives, I gathered a collection of essays, quotes, and student writing that described experiences that profoundly influenced individuals. I wanted students to read these examples before beginning their own short essays. In her book, *I Wanna Take Me a Picture,* Wendy Ewald, a photographer and teacher, shares an experience that changed her approach and philosophy as an artist:

> One day Ewald and a 14-year-old student, Merton Ward, went to photograph the cemetery. Ewald's picture—carefully composed, taken from above—showed what the graveyard looked like. But Merton's—shot from below, looking up at the tombstones—was scarier, more threatening; it made you realize how it felt emotionally to be there, what the cemetery meant for the community, especially for its children. She [Ewald] describes the experience as a "turning point": the moment she understood that "his pictures portrayed reservation life more accurately and expressively than mine." From then on, her work with kids became a collaborative project in which she gave them the skills necessary to realize their own visions—and allowed those visions to directly influence the photographs she took." (2001, 8)

Paul, one of my students from a previous school year, wrote an essay that I shared in this workshop about a turning point in his life as a writer. Paul—a big, street-smart guy—was, unbeknownst to his classmates, friends, and even family, a poet. He reveals these qualities through his turning point essay:

> I remember the first poem I ever wrote for myself, not because I was forced by a teacher to write it, but because I wanted to. I came home from practice late that night and my mom asked where I had been and why I had the huge black eye with the cut on the side of my face. I explained that it was from wrestling practice and I was fine. As I went in my room, I began to wish I could have told her the truth and explain how humiliated I was. But if I had she would worry about me even more than she already did. With all my anger, I began to hit my bed and floor. I broke some CDs and other little things. I imagined it was the older boy who had beat me down and his friend who watched and laughed. My face burned with anger and I felt like I was going to explode. I needed to do something. I remembered someone telling me it feels good to write about your problems and I always thought that was bullshit, but I figured why not try? I began to write and I didn't even write full sentences. The page was full of words that didn't make sense to anyone but me and it was kinda freeing. I wrote about everything going on in my life, first about the boy who humiliated me, then my dad and my home life, then about how I hated my skin color that made me a bit of an outcast at my school. I wrote about how the girls that I was with didn't mean anything and I would give them all up for one girl I could hold. When I was finally done, I looked at the paper through blurry eyes. I felt better. I wanted to rewrite it later 'cause it was saturated in tears and very sloppy. I laid back and felt a heaviness raise off my shoulders. For the first time, I got a good night's sleep.

Paul's honest telling of this turning point as a writer gave students a model of another student who had stumbled upon a life calling. I try to share student writing (along with published pieces whenever possible) as models, and also encourage students to send their own writing out for publication. I often use writing models drawn from previous students' publications to help inspire current students to send their work out into the world. When students see that their peers have written and published thought-provoking essays and poems that are just as powerful as the work of more "accomplished" or famous writers, class projects seem more attainable and relevant. When students are kept at a distance with a curriculum that does not feel connected to who they are as young adults, the relevance of the work remains difficult for them to grasp.

I assigned students a short essay describing a turning point in the life of the activist they were in the process of studying. This workshop was designed to give students a lens into the kinds of experiences that take place in individuals' lives that influence their work as activists. It also gave students a chance to write about, respond to, and analyze their books of choice. The more writing varieties students were exposed to through reading and writing themselves, the more they began to understand the choices we make as writers every time we sit down to write. Stephen King explains the connection he sees between reading and writing in the following way:

> The real importance of reading is that it creates an ease and intimacy with the process of writing. . . . It also offers you a constantly growing knowledge of what has been done and what hasn't, what is trite and what is fresh, what works and what just lies there dying (or dead) on the page. (2000, 150)

Students may begin with the same writing prompt, as they did with the turning point essay; however, I want them to understand through example that their writing choices may be unique to their subject matter and what they choose to share with the audience. I used the prompt in Handout 3.1 for the turning point essay assignment.

Sam wrote about the main character in his book, a teenage girl named Irene who worked to rescue Jews in the Holocaust:

> Irene's turning point came when she chose to leave her home and family and move to a big city to become a nurse. While on her way to the hospital one day to continue her training, the Germans began bombing Poland. She and the other nurses in training were forced to become lifesavers in a matter of minutes. They were crammed into busses and vans and then fled to the forest to get away from the bombs. She was then living among soldiers, wounded men and women, and other nurses in the woods hiding from the Nazis. Soon, they got word that the

Turning Point Essay

Please write a short essay today in class that answers the following questions about the activist in your book:

- What was a turning point in your activist's life?
- How did this event or experience influence this person?
- How did this event contribute to his or her activism work?
- How do you relate to this story?

Due at the end of class

Handout 3.1

Nazis had taken Poland and there was no more Polish army. Irene took what she could carry and walked away. She passed out and awoke in a Russian hospital. The head nurse was very nice and allowed Irene to continue to be a nurse. Irene's decision to become a nurse and help others is the reason she made such a big impact on others.

Diana's essay described Lesley Koplow's experiences with young children and how they shaped Koplow's future decision to become a children's therapist. This essay highlights how role models can profoundly influence people's interests and life aspirations:

Lesley Koplow knew she was going to work with children at the age of eleven. "The kindergarten teacher came into our sixth grade class to ask for two volunteers to work in the kindergarten the first hour of every morning" [Koplow 1990, 4]. She was excited by the importance of the job and also the chance to work with children. The kindergarten teacher who oversaw her early work had a major influence on Lesley. "You should not work with children because you lack the opportunity to do something else, but because you have something special to give, you have a gift" [5]. These words, along with her enjoyable experiences helping children with specific problems, led Lesley to pursue higher education, specializing in children. "By the time I finished my graduate studies in early childhood special education and pediatric social work, I had worked with disturbed and disabled children in recreational, educational, and therapeutic programs and was looking for a job that would allow me to integrate teaching and clinical work" [5].

Armed with lots of knowledge and a heart prepared to give each child his or her all, Lesley began work at the federally funded preschool program in East Harlem. There, she established a playroom where children could explore their dark pasts and learn to deal with the future.

My connection to Lesley's experience helping in a kindergarten room is when I was in fifth grade and had a first-grade buddy. I remember feeling so powerful and grown-up. The little kids looked up to the fifth graders and just by acting or speaking in a certain way, you could easily influence them. My buddy was not disabled or disturbed like the children Lesley worked with. In fact, she came from a loving family whom I met at occasional school functions. Even so, I really enjoyed helping her with art projects, treasure hunts, and reading books.

Experiences like these are priceless. Not only did my buddy benefit from our six-month relationship, but I did as well. I learned a little bit more about the mind of a six-year-old and how she had a lot of ideas that were like my own.

The turning point writing proved to be important in helping students differentiate between issues people *cared* about and issues that they were truly *passionate* about. Jenny wrote about a turning point in Gloria Steinem's life that influenced her work as an activist. The following is a small section of her essay:

> From what I have read so far in my book, Gloria Steinem's biggest turning point would be when she was a campaign officer for McGovern when he was running for president. She thought she was going to be his campaign officer and make speeches and help him with his work. Then she realized this wasn't what he had in mind for her and that she was going to have to work as his slave. She was told to bring him drinks and food and run small errands. He didn't expect much more from her because she was a woman. She decided after this experience that she did not ever want to be that woman again. She wanted to be thought of as a strong human being and an independent woman. So, with that in mind, she took off and decided she would make this happen, not only for herself, but for all women that were being treated the same way. She wanted to have respect and she no longer wanted to be considered the weaker of the two genders. I think that there were other women who have influenced the feminist movement, but the combined work of all these women is what has led to changes in the way women are seen in society. Perhaps without the long chain of events that led to Gloria's epiphany, she would have never decided to act on what she was feeling.

Later, when students were to choose and develop their own activism projects, they had this experience thinking and writing about the turning points of others to help them make a decision about their own projects.

Activism Article

> It is not only important to have hope, but you have to work for that hope. You can't expect everything to turn out how you want

> if you don't work for what you want. Anything can be achieved
> if you strive to get your goals met and your voice heard. (Margo,
> ninth grade)

After students wrote the turning point pieces and as they continued reading their books of choice, they took part in a number of writing workshops to prepare them to write a culminating essay. With a clear sense of the kind of writing I wanted students to practice, I spent time each week teaching skill lessons or assigning specific writing tasks that directly led to this writing goal. Using the activist books of choice, students wrote an expository article about the activist they had studied. The expository genre gave students practice sharing their new knowledge about their selected activist, weaving outside information into their writing, and trying on a new kind of writer's voice that speaks with authority and information. The purpose of these articles was to inform and teach others about the kinds of qualities that make up a successful activist.

I spent time with students introducing them to each writing genre we tackle. In this case, I explained the differences between the expository piece they were about to create and the narrative writing they had completed earlier in the unit (see Chapter 1). I shared how expository writing works to teach and inform the reader about a particular topic. It is important to teach the qualities that make up particular writing tasks and how these qualities serve specific purposes. Often students struggle with writing assignments not because they are weak or struggling writers, but because they are not familiar with the conventions of the particular task. It is my job to demystify the particular qualities and standards for each writing genre we practice so that students are not left in the dark about how to succeed.

I found models of expository essays about activists within Phillip Hoose's *It's Our World, Too!* (2001) along with articles from current newspapers and magazines. I assigned students to bring in an article or articles from newspapers, magazines, flyers, books, or similar sources describing activism work. We created a bulletin board in the classroom that was reserved for "activism in the news." I wanted students to have as much exposure as possible to a wide variety of activism projects as well as the ways writing can be used to inform others about this work. As students brought in articles, we all learned about individuals whom we had not known about previously or originally thought of as activists. We read about a school bus driver in Portland who collects used and abandoned school supplies and sends them to poor villages in Mexico. We examined Sebastian Selgado's famous photos of workers in Brazil and talked about the power of written as well as visual media in expressing ideas and opinions. One morning, Justin announced, "Hey, Ms. Singer, did you see the cover of *Time* magazine [Tyrangiel 2002]? Bono from the rock band U2—he's an activist. His issue is Africa. He's working to try to help relieve debt in Africa. Who knew? That dude never struck me as anything but a rock star before I read about this!" It's always a thrill to witness students absorb new information that they find independently beyond my classroom walls. We also talked about the ways in which the authors of these articles shared information using concise summaries of background information and facts, quotes from multiple authors, primary and secondary sources, and a somewhat formal voice.

By the time students received all of the requirements for this final expository essay, I made sure that they had many chances to generate writing that they could later borrow to draft their essays (see Handout 3.2).

Students practiced specific writing skills through this essay project. They wrote leads, summaries, research logs, personal reflections, and effective conclusions. In order to give students time to learn and practice these skills, I wove together writing lessons to connect with the reading. For example, on the days we read our books of choice silently or practiced reading strategies for the first half of class, I used the second half of class as a time for students to practice their writing and react to what they had just read. Here is an example of the kind of writing prompt I created for one of these kinds of writing lessons:

Writing Prompt 1: Movement Toward Change

What does your activist's story have to teach others that could help move them to work toward making positive social change? Include two to three quotes from this person.

This simple writing prompt asked students to think about their books as enjoyable and entertaining stories as well as examples of

Activism Article

I would like you to write an expository article based on your activist's work toward change. This article will not only teach others about this particular activist, but it will also share what this work has to offer others. Using the writing you have already done (the turning point, timeline, movement toward change, etc.) and new writing, you will write an article to teach others. The article must include

- a title
- a successful lead
- background information
- at least one interesting anecdote about the activist
- at least two quotes from your activist
- a connection to your own life
- a successful conclusion

Due Date: _____

life lessons. Students began to define activism in their own words through the knowledge they had gained from their books. As Matt read Gandhi's autobiography, he discovered some of the qualities an activist embodies and how activism work can start with self-awareness before moving outward to change others:

> Gandhi's autobiography deals a lot with understanding himself. His "quest for truth" is a big theme, and he includes a lot of events in his life that have changed him profoundly. I think, even though Gandhi was an incredible organizer of people, and led the Indian people to independence, that this book is more about change in one's self. "When such *Ahimsa* (love and nonviolence) becomes all-embracing, it transforms everything it touches." In Gandhi's life, he spent a lot of time helping people. In South Africa, he fought and taught other Indians how to fight for their rights. He was a natural teacher and he had an incredible sense of what was right and wrong. I think that the story of his life and his exploration of self inspires others to study themselves, and to see what they can do to become better people.

Margo wrote about her impressions of Ashwari's *This Side of Peace* (1996) and Ashwari's work as an activist in the Middle East. Margo eloquently and succinctly described her understanding of what it means to stand up for one's beliefs:

> It would be difficult to be a Palestinian woman in the middle of an Israeli revolution. For a long time, Israel and Palestine have butted heads. This woman, Hanan Ashwari, had to face the nightmare of having her home taken away. People came to her homeland and suddenly she was discriminated against and treated as an outsider. "You have to face the facts. The Arabs have lost the war. The West Bank, the Sinai, and the Golan Heights are under Israeli control" [20]. Hanan did not let people tell her that she wasn't a good person and she did not sit down and let her homeland be ripped away along with the rights of the Palestinians everywhere. Her story is very inspirational. It teaches us that it is not only important to have hope, but you have to work for that hope. You can't expect everything to turn out how you want it to if you don't work for what you want. Anything can be achieved if you strive to get your goals met and your voice heard. If you make your voice heard, you will also be seen. This unfortunately means you are going to have your every difference, every belief, and every flaw

pointed out and scrutinized. "While I made a place for myself in this new world, acceptance by all was not automatic" [29]. Although, as we see from this book, you cannot give up on your cause when others are not supportive. You have to shrug their criticism off and focus on the main goal, then you will succeed.

This writing workshop, one that took no longer than thirty minutes, gave Margo a chance to articulate her understanding and wisdom about activism work. She also clearly demonstrates within this piece her ability to use textual examples to reinforce her ideas.

Leads

Ralph Fletcher writes, "The first word, sentence, paragraph, or passage—commonly called the lead—represents the author's first step toward finishing a piece of writing. But the lead is more than the first step toward getting somewhere; the lead is an integral part of the somewhere itself" (1992, 82). I wanted students to add to what I call a "tool box of writing strategies" by learning multiple ways of taking the first step in writing a lead. We talked about the importance of first impressions in both writing and reading. I have little patience for a story that does not capture my attention from the get-go. I know there are other readers and viewers who have more staying power; however, as a writer I want to make sure that my words capture my audience's attention and imagination immediately.

In a skill-lesson on "leads," I shared examples of a variety of successful leads from books, articles, and newspapers that I have collected over time. I read from the first page of one of my favorite books of all time, *The God of Small Things* by Arundhati Roy. Roy begins her award-winning novel with a breathtaking description of the weather in the region of India where the story takes place: "May in Ayemenem is a hot, brooding month. The days are long and humid. The river shrinks and black crows gorge on bright mangoes in still, dustgreen trees. Red bananas ripen. Jackfruits burst. Dissolute bluebottles hum vacuously in the fruity air. Then they stun themselves against clear window-panes and die, flatly baffled in the sun. The nights are clear, but suffused with sloth and sullen expectation" (1997, 3). I give students a copy of this passage and ask them to follow along as I read it aloud. When I finish reading, I ask them to reread the paragraph and highlight all of the descriptive language Roy uses to establish the setting and mood. Students begin to see how this author's word choice is intentional and paints a powerful picture with imagery and descriptive language. I also read the lead from Alexandra Fuller's beautiful memoir *Don't Let's Go to the Dogs Tonight* (2003), which is her story of growing up in Africa. She begins the book with dialogue between herself as a child and her parents. I used examples from Ralph Fletcher's chapter on beginnings in *What a Writer Needs* (1992) as well as sample leads from Linda Christensen's *Reading, Writing, and Rising Up* (2000). I asked students then to delve back into the beginnings of their books to see if the stories began with dialogue, setting description, an explanation of a problem, an anecdote, or some other mechanism. I provided examples of different strategies for writing leads from various authors I admire and whose texts I often use in my teaching (see Handout 3.3).

Throughout my teaching, I continually share my own writing and process with students. For example, I was in the middle of writing an article for *Rethinking Schools* (Singer 2002) about my work to untrack my English department when I first taught this minilesson on leads. I shared the "first draft" of the lead for the article with my students, and the experience of my editor saying he thought I needed to go in a different direction. I told students how I loved the first lead I had written and felt attached to these words:

First Draft Lead

The day I was hired at Cleveland High School, my new principal took me on a tour of the hundred-year-old brick building. As a second year teacher, just having moved to Portland, Oregon, I was thrilled to have a job at an urban school in my neighborhood with a reputation for a fabulous English department and an incredible administration. My principal guided me in what felt like circles around the hallways, through the auditorium, library, and finally to the east wing. "Unfortunately," he smiled kindly, "the east wing is kind of a hike to get to each morning. This is the only available classroom." I did not complain. Later that fall, a fellow English teacher informed me that the east wing is referred to as "Siberia." The

Writing the Introduction

A strong opening is crucial if you are to catch your reader's attention. The first several sentences are especially important. You can experiment with the following techniques:

- **Startling or Interesting Facts: An unusual fact can disturb, surprise, or inform your readers or make them curious. Notice how the writer uses the huge number ("one hundred million women") and the startling phrases ("genitally mutilated") to grab the reader's interest.**

  An estimated one hundred million women in African, Asian, and Middle Eastern countries have been genitally mutilated, causing unimaginable physical pain and suffering. And though one is struck by the complicity of the mothers, even the complicity of the grandparents, one must finally acknowledge, as Hanny Lightfoot-Klein does in the title of her book about genital mutilation in Africa, that those who practice it are, generally speaking, kept ignorant of its real dangers—the breakdown of the spirit and the body and the spread of disease—and are themselves prisoners of ritual. (Walker 1993)

- **Vivid, Detailed Description: A graphic, mysterious, or sensory description of a person or place can capture the reader's imagination. Here the author presents a vivid description of the scene on a river boat on the Zaire River.**

  The captain, in crisp white pajamas with baby-blue polka-dots, stalked the bridge. As his boat growled down river through a green-black rainforest, he shouted and whistled and pointed to the deck below. There the beasts that had arrived in the night were being auctioned. Glaring white morning light poured over steaming heaps of mottled fur and squirming legs. It was already hot and the carcasses were ripening. (Harden 1992, 23)

- **Questions: A question can get your reader thinking and wanting to read on to find the answer.**

Handout 3.3

What is she doing, this bewitching young woman of Bali? Moistening her forehead with holy water, then her temples and her chest just below the throat. Now she sticks on a dozen luminously white kernels of uncooked rice. On her copper-colored skin they gleam like jewels. . . . (White 1994)

- **Incidents or Anecdotes: A bit of retelling—of a story or one interesting event—adds human interest that can draw a reader into a piece.**

On the morning that Manute Bol became a man, six of his lower front teeth were gouged out with a chisel. In the afternoon of that same day his head was shaved and rubbed with ashes. He was told to lie down and rest his head on a pillow of wood. Using a sharp knife, a master of the fishing spear cut four incisions, intended to create shallow V-like scars, all the way around his head. He was fourteen years old at the time and very much attached to his teeth, which he cleaned after every meal with a stick. Nor was he keen about having scars on his head. He had been avoiding Dinka manhood rites for years. He ran away from home at the age of eight when tribal tradition demanded removal of teeth. He left home again when he was twelve, the age for ritual scarring. (Harden 1992)

- **Quotations: A quotation can personalize and add interest to a piece of writing. The quotation chosen by this writer provokes our interest in finding out how a wind can cause people to fight.**

"On nights like that," Raymond Chandler once wrote about the Santa Ana, "every booze party ends in a fight. Meek little wives feel the edge of the carving knife and study their husbands' necks. Anything can happen." That was the kind of wind it was. I did not know then that there was any basis for the effect it had on all of us, but it turns out to be another of those cases in which science bears out folk wisdom. The Santa Ana, which is named for one of the canyons it rushes through, is a foehn wind, like the foehn of Austria and Switzerland and the hamsin of Israel. There are a number of persistent malevolent winds, perhaps the best known of which are the mistral of France and the Mediterranean sirocco. (Didion 1990, 14)

Handout 3.3 (continued)

geography of a teacher's classroom matters. The fact that my room was in the back of the building, at the end of an infrequently used hall, beside the door to the back road where students skipped class to smoke and skate, framed my year as a teacher.

I then described how the editor thought that my first lead was well written, but that it did not clearly set up the article's purpose. He wanted me to start over. I shared multiple revisions with students to show how much work it took before I wrote the one that worked for the article and the editor. Students saw the difference between my first draft and my final draft to highlight the hard work in revision and the importance of "letting go" of writing that may not fit with a particular project.

Final Lead

"Just make it through the year," said the teacher sitting next to me at one of the first English department meetings of the school year. "Wait to think about what worked and what didn't until it's all over." And though my colleague was trying to be supportive, his words served as a reminder that many teachers—both new and seasoned—think that a new teacher's major goal is to survive the school year.

I was feeling overwhelmed. I had just been hired as an English teacher at Cleveland High School in Portland, Oregon. I was teaching two freshmen honors classes, two sophomore "regular" classes and one senior honors class. But I didn't want to put my head down and plow through the year, only to look up in June as my students walked away. I wanted to think about what was happening in my classes and in my school.

I decided to approach my year from a place of inquiry—and this grew into an effort to dismantle the tracking system that was in place in our school.

Students were invited into my process of letting go of a lead that was well written, but not perfectly suited to the direction of the article. They learned that revision is part of the process of clarifying how you express yourself in writing and not a sign of failure. Knowing that revision is a helpful process supports students' ability to reflect openly and in an in-depth manner about their own writing.

I asked students to practice writing three to five different kinds of leads of their own to begin the activism articles. I then assigned them to reflect on which of these leads would best suit their articles in progress. Jose chose to use a lead from this workshop in his essay on Muhammad Ali:

"Draft Beer, not Ali"

The paperwork was all filled out. The physical was passed. There was only one more step before the armed forces. The young men were lined up before a young lieutenant, and instructed to step forward when their names were called. They would then become official members of the United States Army. As the lieutenant made his way down the line, each man stepped forward.

"Cassius Clay."

Ali remained silent.

"Ali."

Again, no response.

Severin used a question to begin his lead describing Tom McCall, a famous governor from Oregon:

His Time: The Story of Tom McCall

Have you ever seen such a turn-around from one person? Throughout Tom McCall's childhood, people told him that he was not outgoing enough. Even his mother was worried about him. "What are we going to do, Mr. Johnson, with Tommy? He's just sinking into his shell. He's not grasping the challenges of life at all" [Neal 1977, 2]. Tom McCall changed. As he grew up, whenever he disagreed with something, he stood up and spoke out against it, even if it cost him his career. Tom McCall grew up to be one of Oregon's most influential governors.

Weaving Quotes

After noticing that students were struggling to embed quotes smoothly within their writing, I created a skill-lesson with my friend Ruth, who is a fellow teacher and writer. We were determined to create concrete strategies to teach students how to weave quotes into their articles. This skill is something all writers need to know how to do to write successful nonfiction articles and academic pieces—and one that is sometimes difficult to do well. My friend Ruth and I sat down together and created a handout with helpful hints and practices that we use in our own writing all the time. We tried to make the lesson as concrete and accessible as possible. Handout 3.4 shows the basic rules we came up with and examples from Ruth's writing about Helen Keller (Hubbard 2002) to model the specific strategies.

Students practiced finding effective and interesting quotes as they read their books of choice. I handed out sticky notes for them to mark passages that caught their attention as they read. As they began writing first drafts of their articles, students were increasingly prepared to successfully include quotes within their writing to support their main ideas.

Examples of Embedded Quotes

The Dalai Lama was shocked and saddened to learn of this event. He found it hard to understand why anyone would do this to another person. "When I heard of it, I cried. I could not believe that human beings were capable of such cruelty to each other." (Dalai Lama 1990, 110)

—*Coco*

However, Irene realized that doing the right thing does not come easily. "You must understand that I did not become a resistance fighter, a smuggler of Jews, a defier of the SS and the Nazis, all at once. One's first steps are always small." (Opdyke 1999, 143)

—*Emma*

But not everyone cheered for Hanan. As she recalls, "While I made a place for myself in this world, acceptance by all was not automatic." (Ashwari 1996, 29)

—*Margo*

After Reading a Life Story

To help students write conclusions for their articles, I asked them to respond to a simple prompt when I knew they were close to completing their books of choice.

Tips on Using Quotes

Quotes do not work when they are plunked in—you need to prepare your reader for the quotes you are going to use. Here are some ways to weave your quotes into your writing effectively.

1. Assume your reader knows nothing about your person or subject—provide the right context/background for the quote.

   Helen was a socialist who believed she was able to overcome many of the difficulties in her life because of her class privilege. She concluded, "I owed my success partly to the advantages of my birth and environment. I have learned that the power to rise is not within the reach of everyone."

2. Your quotes should be short and sweet.

3. If you find a perfect quote to illustrate your point but it is too long, there is a way to shorten it without changing the author's words. You can leave three dots . . . to indicate where you have left out words. (See bold example below.)

   "So long as I confine my activities to social service and the blind, they compliment me extravagantly, calling me 'archpriestess of the sightless,' 'wonder woman,' and 'a modern miracle.' **But when it comes to a discussion of poverty, and I maintain that it is the result of wrong economics—that the industrial system under which we live is at the root of much of the physical deafness and blindness in the world—that is a different matter!**"

   "So long as I confine my activities to social service and the blind, they compliment me extravagantly, calling me 'archpriestess of the sightless,' 'wonder woman,' and a 'modern miracle.' **But when it comes to a discussion of poverty, and I maintain that it is the result of wrong economics . . . that is a different matter!**"

Handout 3.4

4. Remember that your words should carry the piece—not your quotes! Quotes should illustrate what you have already said in the essay.

5. There are two ways to begin the writing process when you know you will use quotes.

   a. Write your piece first without quotes and then look for the quotes later that back up what you have written.

   b. Gather quotes that grab your attention and then find a thread or connecting idea within these quotes. Then begin your writing using this idea as your focus.

6. After you finish a draft, read your piece over and see if the quotes move the piece forward. If any bog you down—cut them out!

7. Share your piece with a trusted reader.

8. Have fun writing.

Handout 3.4 (*continued*)

Writing Prompt 2: Movement Toward Change Free Write

What does your activist's story have to offer others that could move them to think differently or work toward change? Include two to three quotes from this person.

Students' powerful responses to this question revealed that they understood the stories of the activists in their books and that they could define activism in relation to their own values and interests. Diana wrote the following in her free write and combined her new words with a paragraph from the turning point essay she had written previously. (The paragraph from the turning point essay is surrounded by a square below.) These two pieces together became the conclusion for Diana's final article about Lesley Koplow, a children's therapist:

Lesley Koplow is not a traditional social activist. She does not stand at the front of a picket line, nor did she have a heart-breaking childhood loss or tragedy. She is one of those remarkable people who found something they love to do and are good at. For Lesley, helping disturbed children from poor inner city families is a passion. Each day when she plays with children, she is not thinking about the world impact or of the enormity of her work. She is focused on the child in front of her, helping her to learn and integrate into life. She helps young people find the root of their mental torture. There was never any question for Lesley about what she was going to do with her time, effort, and devotion.

Lesley's work and influence with children reminds me of being in fifth grade and having a first grade buddy. I remember feeling so powerful and grown-up walking into the first grade classroom. The little kids looked up to the fifth graders and just by acting or speaking a certain way, I could easily influence them. My buddy was not disabled, or disturbed like the children Lesley Koplow worked with. In fact, my buddy came from a very loving family whom I met occasionally at school functions. Even so, I really enjoyed helping her with art projects, treasure hunts, and books. Experiences like these are priceless. Not only did she benefit from our six-month relationship, but I did as well. I learned a little bit more about the mind of a six-year-old, and how her thoughts were a lot like my own.

It is important to make these small discoveries. This kind of learning helps us to better understand ourselves, and use that new information to make positive change in the world. Probably the most significant lesson Lesley Koplow can teach us, is that one person can make so much more of a difference than we allow ourselves to think. You do not need to look at yourself in the mirror and ask what you did for the world that day. Instead, you need to ask yourself what you did to make one person's life better. If you look in the mirror after asking yourself this question and your reflection smiles back, you have found purpose and a way to make a difference.

The above selection from Diana's article serves as an example of how students used each writing workshop to build toward a complete final essay. I encouraged students to find ways to cut and paste their words so that they did not have to reinvent the wheel each time they sat down to write.

Final Articles

As students finished their revision work and their articles were ready to be shared publicly, they took turns in a chair at the front of the room and introduced the class to their activists by reading the articles aloud. Taylor turned to me during class one day to say, "I can't wait to tell people about Cassius Clay. I bet most people in the room have no idea that that was Muhammad Ali's first name, and even better, I bet they didn't know he was an antiwar activist. He's so cool!"

The following is Margo's final article about the Palestinian activist, Hanan Ashwari:

Not for the World

Imagine you cannot see a thing. The windows are painted black. You dare not move. You dare not speak. You dare not breathe. This is what it was like for Hanan Ashwari as she sat huddled in the basement. It was the middle of the Israeli Palestinian War and a man opened the door to the basement and told the group of schoolchildren that Israel had won the war. The West Bank, Gaza Strip, and Golan Heights were now under Israeli rule.

Hanan and her sister tried to digest this information as they squinted at the unfamiliar sights. Their home no longer belonged to them. The home they grew up in, the rooms where birthday parties and holiday celebrations were once held, became a memory shadowed by a blue and white flag.

As a young woman full of determination and spirit, Hanan was destined to do great things. Something clicked inside Hanan at a young age telling her this kind of hatred and segregation was not right. No one person should be treated so poorly. She wanted to see discrimination come to an end.

Though Hanan had aspired to be a doctor, like her father, wise words from her mother led her to teaching. She was an English professor, but her passion was freedom. "From the onset, the occupation and I did not get along" [Ashwari 1996, 31]. Because Hanan was a professor, she was supposed to stay relatively neutral in political matters. As a radical social activist, Hanan attended many rallies and worked after hours on a project to give Palestinian students rights. Though she never did anything violent, Hanan was often charged with such things as civil disobedience and threatening the security of the state. Her colleagues, for the most part, supported her actions. She often found herself bailed out by the university.

But not everyone cheered for Hanan. As she recalls, "While I made a place for myself in this world, acceptance by all was not automatic" [29]. It is the risk you take with the job. If you wish to create positive social change, you are bound to catch some angry comments or hateful looks. Hanan remembers, "At that time the word 'Palestinian' meant terrorist or nothing at all" [30].

Although Hanan spent considerable time working as an activist for the Palestinian people, her attention began to sway toward her growing family. She and her husband, Emile, were now proud parents of Amal and Zeina. Together the family supported Hanan in her daily trips to Jerusalem and helped feed her passion for peace.

I remember when I was in kindergarten and my teacher taught a lesson on discrimination. He let all the kids with blue eyes go out to recess and the rest of us had to stay in and do work. The next day, he let the kids whose last names began with O–Z go outside and, again, the rest of the class had to stay in. I walked up to this teacher and told him that this was not fair and he could not do this to our class. He explained that it was a "real world situation" and he agreed that it was not fair. I was convinced then that the world did not need to be so hateful. From that moment, I knew that discrimination was wrong. Though this is nowhere near what Hanan Ashwari went through I felt as if I have tasted a little bit of what it is like to be an activist. I have had the feeling of a turning point and I firmly believe that some things are right and that other things are wrong. It is the sweetest taste I have ever experienced to stand up for what I believe in. I would not let this feeling go—not for the world.

Margo's activist article not only teaches others about the work of a remarkable activist, Hanan Ashwari, but it shares a sincere connection to this woman's work. Margo reminds me in this essay of the way reading other people's life stories provides opportunities to experience or "taste" new ways of thinking and acting in the world. Through reading and writing about Ashwari, Margo began to form her own understanding of activism—"I firmly believe that some things are right and that other things are wrong."

Students had different reactions to the life stories of the activists they studied. In each case, they expressed the ways in which these stories touched them. Erik wrote in the conclusion of his activism article, "I find it difficult to relate to Rosa Parks' life story because it happened before my birth. I can see that Parks made a difference for all Americans by standing up, or should we say, sitting down on the bus for her beliefs. This book described one person's struggle and moved me to anger as I became aware of the history of unequal treatment in America during the twentieth century." Koko wrote in her activism article how she was drawn to Helen Keller's story because of the differences between Keller's life and her own. "I think Helen and I are different in many ways. This is what caught my attention and captured my interest. It is interesting to know about a life that is totally different than your own. Helen was the type of person who was satisfied and productive in her life even with hardship. I, however, hardly realize what is around me and often find it hard to make the best of things. I often walk away from difficult things instead of working to change them like Helen. Helen did not curse anything for being blind and deaf. I am worried that if this was me I would have cursed life and ran away. I look up to Helen Keller and want to act in my life like she did."

Article Reflections

After students completed their activist articles and before turning in this assignment, I asked them to write a quick reflection letter about what they learned through the experience of writing this piece.

Writing Prompt 3: Article Reflections

Please take time to share what you learned in the process of writing your activist article. What did you notice about your writing process? What did you think about expository writing? What do you like about your article? What do you wish you could spend more time on in your piece? What did you learn about the activist you studied that you will remember?

Reflection letters provide a window into understanding the development and growth of my students from their perspective. Corinne shared how she grew as a writer through this assignment:

When I wrote this article I learned a lot. I learned what background information is. I also learned that if I compare my writing now to the writing I did last year, there is a big difference. I think I have improved. What I notice about my writing process is all the details that go into one essay. What I like about this genre of writing is that there are no limits on what you can write about, but there is a structure that helps. What I like most about my article is my lead. I think it really captures the reader's attention. I wish I could have said even more about Irene Gut Opdyke. She is such an amazing person. I learned from her that no matter what you should never set limits for your life.

Emily wrote the following in her reflection letter:

Dear Ms. Singer,

My writing process was simple. I broke down all of the requirements and completed them one at a time. I started with my lead, then the background, and moved on to finish the anecdote, quotes, and conclusion. When it came to typing my piece I put all of my writing together and added paragraphs to smooth out the transitions.

I found writing an expository piece a little difficult. It was challenging to write all the important parts into the piece without making it sound like a textbook. It was hard to write a piece that would read like a story, but still include all of the criteria.

I really liked the book I read, *In My Hands* by Irene Gut Opdyke. I wanted to write about the shocking events that took place. I hope that in my piece Irene comes off as a brave risk-taker like she is described in the book. My favorite part of my article is the few paragraphs that tell of Irene's encounter with SS officers at the villa where she is hiding her friends. I think that her composure during this situation is shown along with the role of Major Rugemer in her life. It also gives an example of her intelligence and bravery. Irene used her job as the housekeeper of a German major to her advantage. She used the major's position during the war as a way to safely hide her Jewish friends. It wasn't expected that a German major would be smuggling Jews in his home. I like the fact that even though Irene was only a young girl, like me, she found a way to deceive the Nazis! I will always remember that quality about her from this book.

James' article reflection shares what he learned as a writer and as an admirer of Muhammad Ali:

I noticed that when I write, it's best if I take a day off before I edit. Sometimes, the next day I find things to make better that I didn't notice before. I like expository writing because you can use outside sources to help support what you are saying. The part I like best about my piece is my use of dialogue. I think it really helped the piece. I wish I could have gotten a third person to edit my piece. What I learned about Muhammad Ali that I will not forget is how much he gave up to stand up for what he believed in. He gave up his title, passport, boxing license, and millions of dollars because he took a stand against a war he felt was unjust.

These reflections were windows into students' writing processes and development that I would not have access to otherwise. It amazes me to see students adopt the language and strategies of writers and readers when describing their approach to a writing project. Through different kinds of writing, thinking, and discovery, students built a foundation to begin thinking about the kinds of issues that touch their own lives. Students used writing and reflection to define activism on their own terms and demonstrated how significant writing projects are built through meaningful steps connected to one another, leading to polished and thoughtful work.

References

Ashwari, H. 1996. *This Side of Peace*. New York: Touchstone.

Christensen, L. 2000. *Reading, Writing, and Rising Up*. Milwaukee, WI: Rethinking Schools.

Dalai Lama. 1990. *Freedom in Exile: The Autobiography of the Dalai Lama*. San Francisco: Harper.

Didion, J. 1990. *Slouching Towards Bethlehem*. New York: Farrar, Straus & Giroux.

Ewald, W., and A. Lightfoot. 2001. *I Wanna Take Me a Picture: Teaching Photography and Writing to Children*. Boston: Beacon Press.

Fletcher, R. 1992. *What a Writer Needs*. Portsmouth, NH: Heinemann.

Fuller, A. 2003. *Don't Let's Go to the Dogs Tonight: An African Childhood*. New York: Random House.

Harden, B. 1992. *Africa: Dispatches of a Fragile Continent*. New York: HarperCollins.

Hoose, P. 2001. *It's Our World, Too! Stories of Young People Who Are Making a Difference*. New York: Farrar, Straus & Giroux.

Hubbard, R. 2002. "The Truth About Helen Keller." *Rethinking Schools* 17 (1): 10–12.

King, S. 2000. *On Writing*. New York: Scribner.

Koplow, L. 1990. *Where Rag Dolls Hide Their Faces: A Story of Troubled Children*. New York: Dutton.

Mathabane, M. 1995. *Kaffir Boy: The True Story of a Black Youth's Coming of Age in Apartheid South Africa*. New York: Random House.

Neal, S. 1977. *Tom McCall: Maverick*. Portland, OR: Thomas Binford.

Opdyke, I. 1999. *In My Hands: Memories of a Holocaust Rescuer*. New York: Random House.

Roy, A. 1997. *The God of Small Things*. New York: Random House.

———. 2001. *Power Politics*. Boston: South End Press.

———. 2002. *DAM/AGE: A Film with Arundhati Roy*. New York: First Run/Icarus Films.

Singer, J. 2002. "Getting Students off the Track." *Rethinking Schools* 17 (1): 16–17.

Tyrangiel, J. 2002. "Can Bono Save the World?" *Time,* March 4.

Walker, A. 1993. "A Legacy of Betrayal: Confronting the Evil Tradition of Female Genital Mutilation." *Ms* (November/December): 55–57.

White, P. T. 1994. "Rice, the Essential Harvest." *National Geographic Magazine* (May): 46–82.

Songs of Activists

*Unless we hear the work songs, war
songs, love songs, dance songs of all the
people everywhere, we are most apt to lose
the peace and this world along with it.*

—Woody Guthrie

My brother and I attended back-to-back Bruce Springsteen concerts while I was in the middle of teaching this curriculum on activism. The way Springsteen's music resonates with people of varying ages, social classes, and ethnicities caught my attention. His voice and lyrics strike a chord with people and move them to tears, to dance, and to sing along. I thought about the way music is often used in political and empowering ways, such as the hymns sung by slaves in the Underground Railroad and the music used to protest apartheid South Africa. Through their lyrics and sound, musicians serve as powerful social activists. I attended other concerts prior to these two and had witnessed crowds with similar reactions to music. However, these shows took place at the perfect time for me as a music fan and as a teacher. I realized that I often leave music out of my curriculum even though it is a form of expression that my students appreciate greatly and immerse themselves in daily. I began to consider the ways in which this art form serves as a compelling mode of activism as well as a way to further deepen our studies.

After staying up too late for two nights in a row listening to Springsteen and the E-Street Band with my ecstatic brother, I returned to my classroom Monday morning and shared stories about the concerts with students. I talked about how many of Springsteen's recent songs were written as a reaction to 9/11. Springsteen shared a story of going to the New Jersey shore with his kids. He explained that he was backing his car out of a parking lot when a man in an adjacent car leaned out and told Springsteen, "We need your music now more than ever." This stranger's words inspired Springsteen to create a new album of songs as a way of responding to horrible violence and injustice. Students shared stories of their own about being truly moved and inspired by the messages in musicians' lyrics. Eric shared how he went to a rap concert at a nearby college. He grinned as he told the class how he had enough nerve to get up on stage with the musicians and rap along with them. "It was so killer! I have never been so nervous and so inspired all at once! It's a way of expressing myself that gets me so fired up!" I started to think about the ways in which music not only resonates with individuals, but how it can also serve as a call to action. Howard Zinn describes the role of artists, particularly musicians, as agents of powerful change. "Artists play a special role in social change. I first noticed this when I was a teenager and becoming politically aware for the first time. It was people in the arts who had the greatest emotional effect on me. I'm thinking primarily of singers: Pete Seeger, Woody Guthrie, Paul Robeson . . . It seemed to me that artists had a special power when they commented, either in their own work or outside their work, on what was happening in the world. There was a kind of force they brought into the discussion that mere prose could not match" (Barsamian 2004, 4–6). I created a "songs of activism" workshop as a way to give students an opportunity to bring music into class that mattered to them and also could help them think about activism in new ways.

In this simple and rewarding lesson, students studied songs of activism from historical and contemporary musicians and then brought their own examples of inspirational activism songs to class. This workshop incorporates writing, research, reflection, and discussion—and helps students further define activism in relation to their own interests.

Musicians as Activists

I introduced the songs of activism workshop by sharing an article I found in the *New York Times* about a controversy that took place at a concert by The Dixie Chicks in London, England, at the beginning of the current war with Iraq (Race 2003, 9). Natalie Maines, the lead singer of The Dixie Chicks, made a comment to the audience that the band was embarrassed to be from Texas, the same state as President George W. Bush. The audience cheered and the concert continued into late evening. However, within the next four days—with the help of conservative blogs on the Internet—The Dixie Chicks' comment was all over U.S. newspapers, television, and radio. An argument ensued that the band is anti-American and people should stop buying their music. Even though The Dixie Chicks experienced a dramatic loss in sales during this controversy, they were unwavering in the choice to express their political beliefs in public forums. This news article served as an excellent entry into a conversation with students about the role music and musicians play in provoking political conversations and actions. I purposely chose to keep the focus of this workshop on musicians as activists, rather than choosing a particular kind of protest music or a historical event that inspired this kind of creative resistance. Once again, I wanted to give students a chance to explore multiple forms of activism connected to their own interests.

I shared excerpts from a letter Bruce Springsteen wrote to the *New York Times* on August 5, 2004, which explained his decision to work with other artists to influence the 2004 presidential election. He shared the connection between his work as a musician and his role as a political activist. "A nation's artists and musicians have a particular place in its social and political life. Over the years I've tried to think long and hard about what it means to be American, about the distinctive identity and position we have in the world, and how that position is best carried. I've tried to write songs that speak to our pride and criticize our failures." (Springsteen 2004, A23). Springsteen joined other musicians such as the Dave Matthews Band, Pearl Jam, R.E.M., The Dixie Chicks, Jurassic 5, James Taylor, and Jackson Browne in a tour across the country called "Vote for Change."

I read these articles aloud to students and then asked them if they believe it is appropriate for musicians to use their art form to impact change in the world. Students formulated their thoughts first through writing and then in a class discussion. Spencer raised his hand and said, "I think bands have every right to say what's on their minds. I mean, we pay a lot of money for concert tickets and CDs and we have to be informed about the musician's opinions before we enter the concert stadium." Jordan disagreed: "I am sick of hearing entertainers tell me what they think and who to vote for. I go to concerts to be entertained, not to sit through lectures about boring stuff." Margo cut in, saying that "I think it's great. These musicians and famous people have a lot of people's attention, and if they choose to make their opinions known, then that's their right. The audience doesn't have to do what the artist says. Come on!" As the discussion progressed, I pointed out how volatile certain issues are (such as whether or not to go to war) and how there are often ramifications for standing up for your ideas. We talked about the ways in which music can serve as a medium for expressing opinions about social matters. Chris wrote the following in response to our discussion: "Celebrities have every right to work as activists and they can use that right at their will. They need to realize that being an activist is not the same as a celebrity. These are two different jobs. As a celebrity, a star may be worshipped, but as soon as you transition to an activist role, stars must realize they will get everything that comes along with stating their opinions." Brittany used her written reflection to incorporate her reaction to Michael Moore's public statement against the current administration in his acceptance speech at the 2003 Academy Awards. Brittany explained, "There is a time and a place for anyone to express their opinions. I am strongly opposed to celebrities using their concerts, awards shows, and other public events to state opinions about politics. When I am watching the Academy Awards, I do not want to hear who hates our president. However, if Michael Moore were to win an award for his film, *Fahrenheit 9/11*, he has more of a right to say something political because this coincides with his movie. If celebrities want to make these comments out of context, then they should join political groups and make these comments there." This conversation allowed students to share diverse opinions about the topic and provided a nice bridge into thinking about the ways musicians may influence others through their lyrics as well as through their speeches or nonmusical actions.

Songs of Activism

> Music touches people on a personal level. Music has power, more power than just words alone. It has the power to influence people. Music puts the problem in front of people directly and inspires the listener to work to make positive change. (Margo, ninth grade)

In order to model examples of activism songs, a friend and I went through our CD collections and found two songs to share with students that were written and sung by two of our favorite musicians, Tracy Chapman and Woody Guthrie. Both of these artists are famous for their songs of resistance. Tracy Chapman's "Why" describes what it is like to live in poverty and to be forgotten in this country. The song begins with the following questions: "Why do the babies starve when there is enough food to feed the world? Why when there's so many of us are there people still alone? Why are the missiles called peacekeepers when they are aimed to kill?" We also found Woody Guthrie's famous folk song "Deportee," which describes a plane that crashed and killed Mexican workers who were being deported back to Mexico. Guthrie wrote this song as a form of protest because he was appalled by the newspaper coverage of this event where only the names of the white pilot, copilot, and stewardess were printed. The names of the Mexican workers were left out of the story. In his song, Guthrie gives these individuals names: Juan, Rosalita, Jesus, and Maria. I typed the lyrics of each of the songs and copied them for students to read over once before I played the songs on the stereo.

When I played Woody Guthrie's "Deportee," I asked students what it meant to be deported. Manuel, who is Latino and had recently transferred to Oregon from San Diego, changed the course of this conversation. At first, students shared their opinions about Guthrie's lyrics. One student explained that she thought there was not enough land for everyone, and that is why it is important to send migrant workers back home. Another student quickly applauded this response. The room fell silent. Manuel slowly raised his hand. He said, "These are people without social security. They get kicked out." This was the first time Manuel had spoken up in class. He is often shy and introverted. He moved to Portland in the middle of the school year from San Diego because, as he explained, "I was getting into too much trouble." Manuel's family in southern California worked as migrant farmers and Woody Guthrie's song resonated with his life experience. No other students knew what social security was, other than a number they had to memorize. Manuel explained its meaning for all of us.

I played each song twice so students could listen carefully and read the lyrics for meaning as well. After we heard each song as a class, I handed out a sheet with two questions (see Handout 4.1). These questions were designed to give students an opportunity to reflect on the music in relation to the books of choice they were reading about activists. I did not know if the music's meaning in relation to the unit would make sense to students right away; however, the connections students made between the song lyrics and their books surprised me.

Derek wrote a strong reaction to Woody Guthrie's song and compared its meaning to the book he was reading about Rosa Parks. He wrote, "The connection this song makes to my book about Rosa Parks is that the Americans treat the Mexican workers the same way they treated Rosa. They treated Rosa like a piece of furniture and they did the same with the Mexicans." Spencer, who is Mexican American, also responded strongly to "Deportee." "When I hear this song, I hear the pain my people feel from deportation and from hate. The world has hate for people who do not mirror their image or speak the same language." Diana's response to "Deportee" shared a connection she made between Guthrie's song and reading for another class. "This song reminds me of articles I've read about discrimination in our country and how migrant workers are often deported. My social activism book talked a little bit about immigrant families and how they were trying to start a new life by coming to the U.S., but ended up living in the city scrambling to hold jobs. My major connection to this song is through the movie *Quincenera*, which we saw in Spanish class. It discusses an illegal family's fight to stay in the country and how they are harassed by immigration officials." It is always rewarding when students make connections between what we study in class and their learning in other places. It seems impor-

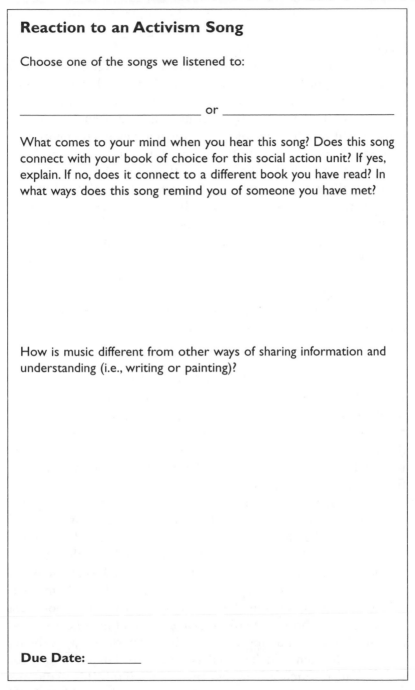

Reaction to an Activism Song

Choose one of the songs we listened to:

_____ or _____

What comes to your mind when you hear this song? Does this song connect with your book of choice for this social action unit? If yes, explain. If no, does it connect to a different book you have read? In what ways does this song remind you of someone you have met?

How is music different from other ways of sharing information and understanding (i.e., writing or painting)?

Due Date: _____

Handout 4.1

tant that a curriculum provide these kinds of bridges for students so that learning relates to the world lying beyond the classroom walls.

Students made interesting connections between books they were reading or had read previously and Tracy Chapman's song, "Why." Emma wrote, "This song connects to the book I read, *In My Hands*. In the song, Tracy confronts issues such as world poverty and war. In the book I read, the main character helps Jews who are facing poverty, death, and war. In the song, after Tracy explains each problem, she explains the irony of each issue. For example, there are starving kids, yet there is enough food to feed the world. In my book, the main character realizes that there is no need to kill her Jewish friends and uses the resources that the Germans are ignoring to save them." Taylor compared Chapman's song to his book about Muhammad Ali. "In Tracy's song, it says, 'But somebody's gonna have to answer, the time is coming soon . . . and the speechless speak the truth.' Those words connect with Muhammad Ali and how he refused to fight in the Vietnam War and spoke out as a conscientious objector."

Eric did not compare Chapman's song to his book of choice, but instead wrote an impassioned response to her lyrics. "I think that 'Why' asks questions that need to be asked by the U.S. I think that 'Why' relates to the music I listen to by Rage Against the Machine. It asks questions that we should know the answers to, but we don't. We don't know that we are safe in our homes. We don't know why we need to keep the peace with force. We don't know why we waste so much and let people die. We should know the answers to these things."

After listening to and discussing Chapman's and Guthrie's songs, I assigned students to collect lyrics from activism songs of their choice. I handed out an assignment sheet with a brief explanation of the task (see Handout 4.2) and asked that they choose songs they were familiar with and that connected to the activism theme. Vanessa's face lit up: "I have so many CDs at home that will work. This is awesome! What happens if I can't choose just one song, can I bring in two?" I gave students time in class to go to the library and look up lyrics. There is a website, www.sing365.com, which served as a wonderful digital library for students to research and access musicians' lyrics. I let students bring as many songs as they wanted to the final sharing workshop,

An Invitation to Music

Songs are powerful tools to build understanding, and they are an important part of social action movements. Some songs bring out the stories and struggles of people whose voices have been left out. Some are songs of resistance, a way for oppressed peoples to show their anger and their solidarity. Some are tributes to struggle and others are songs of activism.

This is an assignment to bring in a song of social change to share with the class. It can be an older song, or one performed by one of your favorite groups that you listen to now. Try to bring in a copy of the lyrics. We won't be able to play all of the songs due to limited class time; however, we will hear a sample from the collection you bring to class.

Due Date: _____

but I only required one. Due to limited time, students could share one song with the whole class.

On the morning of the workshop, Diana, Emily, and Margo all arrived before the bell in their sweatshirts, jeans, and flip-flops and talked together about their song choices. Victor walked into the room and said, "Ms. Singer, the librarian didn't let me download my song lyrics." Victor was absent the day we had gone to the library to look at lyrics and the rule at Cleveland is that students are not allowed to surf the Internet in the library for songs without a note from the teacher. I told Victor that he would have to get the lyrics at another time. I asked him if he was familiar enough with the song he wanted to share to describe it to the class without the lyrics. He nodded and sat down at his desk and later enthusiastically joined the class discussion. I believe it is important to find creative, nonpunitive ways to include students who typically arrive in class unprepared to participate.

When class started, we arranged the chairs in a circle and I set up the stereo in the front of the room. Each student had an opportunity to share the name of the song, a section of the lyrics, and the reasons for choosing the song. Jordan was the first to share. "The name of my song is 'What's Going On,' by Marvin Gaye. I chose this because I think he is talking about the Vietnam War and how a lot of people were protesting but, at the same time, a lot of people weren't listening. This song reminds me of what is happening now with the war in Iraq. A lot of people don't agree that we are over there. I like how this song puts words to that feeling."

I did not require uniformity in student responses. The rule in my class is that everyone needs to participate, but that each student may choose how to share in a way that feels safe. During the songs of activism workshop, Jenna compiled a CD with several songs. When it was her turn to share either a song or the lyrics, she described her collection of protest songs but did not feel comfortable playing them for the class. Jordan tried to pressure her to share the CD with everyone: "Come on Jenna, don't be so shy and wimpy. We want to hear what you put together." Jenna did not want to share her work, and instead gave me the CD and asked that I play the songs later—not in class. Instead of pushing Jenna to choose one of the songs to play as the other students had, I said, "Fine, I'll look forward to hearing it on my own." I try to act as an advocate for students who feel uncomfortable. In this instance, I stressed that Jenna was sharing in a different way and that was fine. As the unit progressed, Jenna's apprehensiveness changed as she started to feel safer in the community that we built over the term. In the final gallery project, which is described in the following chapter, she stood in front of the class and proudly read a poem she had written about unfair labor practices.

Brittany shared the impact of a band's music on her choice to be a vegan. "I have been influenced by Goldfinger. The band members are vegans and they used their music to express their opinions against meat and people like Ted Nugent. Through their music and concerts, I had a door opened for me. The band's songs expressed their opposition to meat, and even insulted some celebrities who wear fur coats. Goldfinger has successfully used their music to educate people about the truth behind the meat industry and I admire this work." Anya described the role of two bands in her life. "For me, there are two music groups that I can say truly made me think about my social and political views. First, Nirvana. When I was younger, Nirvana's music really pushed me to think about authority. Nirvana's music taught me to form my own opinions instead of just blindly accepting the 'normal' or 'right' opinion. Second, Eminem really taught me—or at least made me think about—free speech and why Americans are so scared to expose their children to different ideas." Jeff shared the powerful effects of hip-hop music. "Music has always been a central part of my own development of self and identity. When I first heard Public Enemy and the power of hip-hop music, I just flipped out. I remember that I kept hearing the name *Malcolm X* in Public Enemy songs so one day I went to the library and checked out a copy of the autobiography of Malcolm X."

Not every student felt that music served as a medium for activism work. Annie wrote in her reflection after this workshop that "music, to me, is solely for entertainment purposes. I don't believe music has influenced my political beliefs, unless it has been done discreetly without my awareness. However, music groups committed to political causes have influenced me. For example, MTV has a campaign, 'Rock the Vote,' to encourage young adults to become active and vote. I have used this campaign to educate myself and learn more about the topic so I can develop my own opinions." Jaime explained that "music has never influenced my opinions about politics or anything else really. I love to listen to music but I never really go for the deeper meaning. I listen to country and pop and rap sometimes. But, most of the time, these songs are about love or something, so I never really thought about what they are saying. I usually just think, 'What a cute song.' I also think I have never, until now, really sat down and thought about what an artist is saying." For students like Jaime, I hope that the opportunity to "sit down and think about what the artist is saying" might offer her a new way of thinking about music using a critical lens.

The songs of activism workshop was a simple yet powerful way for students to dig deeper into their thinking about the work of activists. This workshop highlighted the power of music as a way of expressing political and social convictions. The level of enthusiasm for this project was impressive and reminded me of the importance of inviting popular culture into my curriculum in relevant ways. When students shared their songs, Derek had a grin from ear to ear and swayed back and forth in his chair. Jordan became the disc jockey for students who had made CDs. Students sat in a circle and shared with one another their reasons for choosing particular songs. This experience deepened the sense of community and helped create a foundation for the culminating project. One of the things I have noticed about young adults is that it is often difficult for them to stand strongly behind their ideas and to clearly express their beliefs without practice. Often students react to a short story or chapter from a book with comments like "This is awesome!" or "This sucks!" I work hard throughout the school year to teach students to defend their beliefs with reasoning, evidence, and conviction. The songs of activism workshop served as a nonthreatening and enjoyable opportunity for students to publicly articulate the reasoning behind their song choices. This workshop brought students steps closer to the culminating project for the unit as a whole, which was to create and present an activist project of their own.

Songs of Activists: A List in Progress

Action is the antidote to despair. —*Joan Baez*

Artist's Name	Song Title	Subject
The Clash	*Know Your Rights*	Police Brutality
Rage Against the Machine	*Testify*	Call to Action
Creedence Clearwater Revival	*Fortunate Son*	Vietnam War Protest
Black Star	*Brown Skin Lady*	Black Pride
Nas	*I Can*	Empowerment
Faith Evans and Twista	*Hope*	Hope for Change
Wyclef Jean	*If I Was President*	Antiestablishment
Peter Gabriel	*Biko*	Tribute to an Activist
Buffalo Springfield	*For What It's Worth*	War Protest
Public Enemy	*Fight the Power*	Social Injustice
The Doors	*Five to One*	Vietnam War Protest
Eminem	*Mosh*	Iraq War Protest
Tracy Chapman	*SubCity*	Poverty
Crosby Stills Nash and Young	*Ohio*	Kent State Massacre
Cat Stevens	*Peace Train*	Peace
U2	*Sunday Bloody Sunday*	War Protest
Iris Dement	*Wasteland of the Free*	Inequity and Corruption
Axl Red	*Ma Priere*	Globalization
John Lennon and Paul McCartney	*Give Peace a Chance*	Peace
Ben Harper	*Oppression*	Oppression
Bob Marley and Peter Tosh	*Get Up, Stand Up*	Call to Action
Common	*The Corner*	Black Power
Sinéad O'Connor	*Black Boys on Mopeds*	Racism
Bob Dylan	*The Times They Are a-Changin'*	Call to Action
Billy Bragg	*Never Cross a Picket Line*	Pro-Union
Cherry Poppin' Daddies	*Master and Slave*	Poverty
John Mellencamp	*Peaceful World*	Peace
Black Eyed Peas	*Where's the Love*	Peace
Ani DiFranco	*Subdivision*	Inequity and Poverty

Artist's Name	Song Title	Subject
Jadakiss	Why	Poverty and Racism
Marvin Gaye	What's Going On	Vietnam War Protest
No Doubt	Just a Girl	Feminism
Woody Guthrie	Deportee	Immigration
Tracy Chapman	Why	Poverty
Sweet Honey and the Rock	More Than a Paycheck	Migrant Workers' Rights
Michael Franti	Bomb the World	Antiwar
Steve Earle	Christmas in Washington	Plea for Activism
Pearl Jam	Masters of War	Antiwar
Joni Mitchell	Big Yellow Taxi	Environmentalism
Paul Simon	Diamonds on the Souls of Her Shoes	Class Struggle
R.E.M.	Fall on Me	Environmentalism
Lenny Kravitz	Mr. Cab Driver	Racism
Utah Philips	Solidarity Forever	Pro-Union
Bruce Springsteen	The Ghost of Tom Joad	Working-Class Struggle
Johnny Cash	The Ballad of Ira Hayes	A Commentary on the Treatment of Native Americans
John Lee Hooker	The Motor City Is Burning	Detroit Riots
Barry McGuire	Eve of Destruction	War Protest
Pete Seeger	Little Boxes	Consumption of Land
Billy Bragg and Wilco	The Unwelcome Guest	Equity
Vanessa German	Thank You	Antiestablishment

References

Barsamian, D. 2004. "The Role of Artists in a Time of War: An Interview with Howard Zinn." *Sun Magazine* 34 (3): 4–6.

Race, T. 2003. "Most Wanted: Drilling Down Music." *New York Times*, March 24, C9.

Springsteen, B. 2004. "Chords for Change." *New York Times*, August 5, A23.

Songs of Activism Workshop Outline

1. Introduce songs of activism using a current news article or event that illustrates how musicians use their work to express political opinions.
2. Discuss the role of music to influence public opinion as a whole class. Should musicians use their work as a form of activism? Why or why not?
3. Share examples of songs of protest to familiarize students with specific songs that fit this genre (i.e., Woody Guthrie's "Deportee" and Tracy Chapman's "Why").
4. Respond to music with writing (see Handout 4.1: Reaction to an Activism Song).
5. Assign students to bring in an example of a song of activism that resonates with them (see Handout 4.2: An Invitation to Music).
6. Students share songs of activism as a class. Each student shares the name of the song, the artist or group, a brief summary of the song, and a selection of the lyrics. If students bring in a CD or tape, listen to part of it.

Culminating Project
Choosing Issues of Activism

Making Choices as Activists

When I listen to my students' conversations, stresses, and obsessions, I am often reminded of my own adolescence. I spent painful hours as a high school student worrying about silly things like my haircut or finding perfect jeans. I was regularly consumed with anxiety about what other people thought of me. It often astounds me that I chose to become a high school teacher when those years were so miserable. Developmentally, my students are not always walking through their days with wide eyes debating the latest news from abroad or homelessness and hunger here in Oregon. They—like many adolescents—are often consumed with Friday night games and dances, dating, music, and sports. At fifteen, I too found it difficult to recognize or think about a world that lay outside of my immediate range of vision. However, I remember the teachers and mentors who gave me opportunities to think and act beyond my experience and reminded me of the power of small, yet significant, acts. I want to believe that it is not naïve or short-sighted for my students to have an abundance of skills, ideas, and questions to carry with them in their lives in order to influence the world for the better.

I designed the final activism project as an opportunity for students to dive into an issue and project that mattered to them deeply. I wanted to give students an opportunity to use what they had learned through all their hard work surrounding this unit to become both experts and teachers about a particular issue. Although I had hinted at and talked about the final project from the beginning of the unit, I formally introduced the culminating activism project two weeks before the scheduled final for the class at the end of May. First, I gave students time through writing and conversations to brainstorm their own interests as potential activists. I assigned articles about other young adults committed to activism work. I had students return to a section of the wonderful book by Phillip Hoose titled *We Were There, Too!* (2001), a collection of stories of young adult activists in history. This text served as a terrific resource for students exploring their own progressive change interests. One chapter tells the story of Jessica Govea (a young union organizer) while another shares the story of John Tinker (a young war protester). I assigned students a couple of the chapters to read in class and for homework, and I kept this book available as a classroom resource for students to use to gather ideas and inspiration from other young activists. We continued to collect articles from recent newspapers and magazines that told stories of young activists. I offered extra credit when students brought in articles they had found connected to our work. I informed students of local events and author readings about activist issues. My continual aim was to saturate students with information about—and models of—successful activist work. Through these examples, students were reminded that this kind of dedication and interest often grows out of everyday experience.

Final Project Setup

I asked students to create a project to teach others about how to make positive change in their area of concern for needed activism. I wanted students to go beyond a presentation that said, "This issue bothers me." Instead I wanted them to explore their issue indepth through interdisciplinary research. I required that the projects not only share information about their issue in an accessible way, but also that it offer solutions or suggestions for change. Rather than reporting, the projects were meant to inform others about particular issues and then offer original ideas and suggestions for ways people may become directly involved. The plan was to share these final projects in a public gallery format, much like an art gallery, where student work would be displayed in imaginative and creative ways. Students had a great deal of freedom in the creation of these final projects. They could use any media at all as long as they accomplished the goal of educating others. Although students only had a limited amount of time to choose and learn about an issue that mattered to them, all the previous work of the unit served as a foundation for their thinking and helped them make choices about this final task. Students researched their activism topics with the aim of becoming "experts" on these issues.

Some students, like Mary and Coco, knew right away that they wanted to focus their work on funding for libraries and deforestation. However, others—like Nate, Kenzo, and Carla—had a harder time honing in on a specific interest. I encouraged students to brainstorm on issues that mattered to them deeply. We discussed and reviewed all the examples of activists in the books of choice and how activists often find causes they are committed to when the issue impacts them directly. I asked students to brainstorm their hobbies, favorite hangouts, and everyday lives to begin to unveil the places or people they could affect positively by taking action. We talked about the importance of recognizing and valuing seemingly "small" acts. Activism work starts from the kinds of activities and relationships we encounter every day rather than from distant "larger than life" causes. I also gave students a handout, "Teaching to Promote Positive Change," to help them start brainstorming and articulating ideas for the culminating project (see Handout 5.1).

Spencer started brainstorming about discrimination and stereotypes. Eric wrote about his concern for the environment: "I am interested in environmental issues and I want to create a sophisticated political cartoon. I feel strongly about how the government views the environment. I think that we have destroyed enough of our environment but all the government can think of is how to make more money drilling for oil or how to get funding for their campaigns. I think I will make a political cartoon with a

Teaching to Promote Positive Change

Based on the work we have done for this unit on activism and your own interests, what is something you want to help people understand differently (for example, stereotypes about teens, incorrect information about the homeless, faulty images of schools, mistaken beliefs about skateboarders, etc.)? In other words, how is something seen that you don't agree with and why?

How can you teach a new way of seeing or understanding this issue that can promote positive change?

You will create a statement that is visual, oral, written, or musical. This statement will teach your message to an audience.

You will create an artist statement to explain your final project and you will display this along with your project at the final gallery.

Due Date: _____

Handout 5.1

cityscape in the background and someone who is pulling the plug on some wetlands." Danny described his plans for a project about skateboarding: "I think I'll be writing about skaters being treated like crap. I don't see the logic behind being so stupid to skaters. The stereotype skater is the guy who steals stuff, smokes weed, wears baggy pants and a cap. There is a lot more to us than this kind of stereotype shows. I want to teach people the good qualities of skating and how this hobby can be a positive force."

Chelsea decided to focus her project on animal testing and made plans to create a sculpture to teach others about this issue. In Sarah's initial plan for her final activism project she wrote, "I want to choose school funding as my issue because I really believe schools should get more money and support. Another reason why I want my topic to be on poor funding for schools is because I want to be a teacher when I get out of college. If schools are going downhill so fast, by the time I get out of college, there will be nothing good left. I want to make a two-voice poem with a kid in the public school as one voice and an adult figure who has something to do with politics as the other voice. I want to take pictures to illustrate my poetry of the school and what it's really like with such little funding." Sarah's interest in teaching compelled her to focus on school funding. More than one student chose to focus on this topic because the ramifications of budget cuts in Oregon schools were glaringly obvious.

James described his commitment to cleaning up the Columbia River: "An issue that has been bothering me lately is how they are going to dredge the Columbia River again. Environmental agencies working for the government just said it was OK with them. They said it poses no danger to any species, but I find that hard to believe. I would like to do a little research and figure out what is really going on. Do these environmental agencies say it is safe to dredge because it is, or because the government is paying them? I want to write a letter to the government and create a collage, but I am still not positive that is what I will create." Amy is passionate about reducing gang violence. Laurie and Carlos care about the severe budget cuts in Oregon, and how this will affect school funding. Mary is passionate about finding more support for libraries. John and Lisa are concerned about unlawful and unjust labor practices. Clear-cutting and deforestation throughout Oregon enrage Kelly. Carson wants to see skateboarders treated better by adults. Matt is fascinated by and supportive of stem cell research. The range of interests and issues in the classes was broad and sophisticated as can be seen from the lists below.

Period 1

Student Name	Activism Topic
Jenni	Fight for a Cure to Breast Cancer
Matt	Stem Cell Research
Margo	Discrimination Among Teens
Jordan	Religious Tolerance
Emma	Teaching Tolerance
Lisa	Unfair Labor Practices
Danika	Discrimination Among Teens
Corinne	School Funding
Sam	Helping to Stop Racism
Diana	Tolerance
Jose	Against Gangs
Justin	Improving Treatment of Skaters
Erik	Environmentalism
Kenzo	Protecting Endangered Species
Paul	Keeping Oceans Clean
Nate	Improving Skateboarding Facilities
Ken	Teaching Against Racism in Schools
Chelsea	Animal Testing
Veronica	Reducing Gang Violence

Period 2

Student Name	Activism Topic
Carson	Improving Treatment of Skaters
Taylor	Improving Treatment of Skaters
Spencer	Discrimination
Coco	Deforestation
Jeremy	Helping the Homeless
Sarah	Public School Funding
Sean	Teaching Tolerance Through Music
Leigh	Clear-Cutting in Oregon's Old-Growth Forests
Mary	Public Library Funding
Lisa	Poverty in Oregon
Justin	Feeding the Hungry in Portland

Eric	Public School Funding
John	Unfair Labor Practices
Rachel	Public School Funding
Brandon	File Sharing
James	Columbia River Cleanup
Erin	Animal Protection
Danny	Improving Treatment of Skaters
Ben	Incomplete Project

Becoming Experts

Corinne arrived in class one morning with her two-voice poem about poverty and inequity. She said, "Ms. Singer, this is only a piece of what I plan to do, I am wondering if you can edit it for me. I plan to do a multimedia project with this poem as a centerpiece." Students began to sound like experts. Justin and Danny were drawing political cartoons for their projects on skateboarding. These two students never worked so diligently on anything all year until the very last minute or, often, after the fact. To see them finish a week ahead of schedule was thrilling. Spencer plotted a slide show. He asked, "What are those color photos that go up on the screen? That's what I want to make for my project." I gave students two weeks to research, design, write about, and present their final activism projects. Class time during these two weeks was devoted to helping students succeed with their work. The classroom became a workshop space where students sketched out designs for their projects, cut and pasted images from pictures onto poster board, wrote poetry, used computers to research their topics, received revision suggestions from myself and other students, and continually checked in with me about their progress.

During these class sessions, desks were cluttered with poster paper, magazine clippings, glue sticks, highlighters, and drafts of poems, letters, and essays. I expected that some of the work for this project would take place at home, but I also knew that many students would not succeed if I used class time to focus on other things. A teacher I admire greatly once told me that "if you believe something is important enough to teach, then you should teach it in class rather than leaving students on their own to struggle." I've come to believe strongly in this advice. If material feels important and relevant, then I devote time to it in class. I call this kind of class work "inside time." What I love about this informal label for time in class to read, write, revise, plan, organize, and focus is that it reminds me of the way a classroom can become an exhilarating creative space. "Outside time," or time outside of class, was meant to extend and further the work that happened each day in class. I gave students passes to go to the library and research their topics. I gave them access to a phone to make local calls to contact experts who could help inform their projects.

In this time of increasingly standardized testing mandates in education, it is important to find ways to meet state standards and prepare students for achievement tests—while also allowing them to examine their own interests and participate in rigorous and creative work that not only meets standards but exceeds them. I realized that there is a great deal of trust that takes place in this kind of teaching and learning environment. I had to put aside my urge to control, organize, and clean the classroom during these final weeks. Not only did I need to trust students regarding the topics they chose, but also I had to trust that they would each take different routes in accomplishing this work. One student, Jenna, changed her mind about her topic three times before she found her focus. Gabe missed three or four days in the first week of planning the final due to illness. In order to make up this time, he met with me every day for a week during his study hall to catch up with his project plans.

I continually set high standards but decided not to require uniformity in the final creations. This choice felt true to the kind of work that activists immerse themselves in. Individuals work on causes that they have a passion for or investment in, and then the role they take in supporting this cause is connected to their interests, skills, and support. If I had asked every student to choose an issue they loved and then created a uniform project for all of the issues, such as a letter to a politician or an argument essay, then the opportunity for students to become invested in their own kind of change work would have been lost. Once again, I tried to find a balance here between allowing students freedom and choice with these projects while also providing clear expectations, guidance, and reinforcement so that they would not be left to flounder without support.

Checking In

Most mornings I arrived in my classroom early to lay papers on the desks, which explained or set up the assignments for the day. I sharpened pencils and left them in a blue vase by the sink. I wrote, "This is what you need today," with a list of supplies, books, or projects on the chalkboard. I continually updated the "table of contents" list hanging on the wall each morning so students could keep their portfolios current and organized. I learned how this kind of setup, prep, and check-ins with students works to create fewer struggles in our time together and sets them up to focus on the important work of the class. I met with each student briefly every class to check in on his or her progress. These miniconferences took place while students were busy working on their posters, writing, and research. I wandered around the room from student to student and asked where they were in the production process. These quick check-ins helped me monitor and assess students' needs. I discovered the kinds of supplies they needed in order to complete their projects and did my best to provide these. I made copies before and after class for some students, edited two voice poems, gave interviewing advice, purchased slide film, sharpened color pencils, and provided research tips.

When I met with Spencer about his final project, he told me about his plan to create a slide show about tolerance for differences in high school. He wanted to take pictures of all different students in hallways and classes and then he hoped to create a soundtrack for his slide show with songs and poetry about tolerance. When I met with Spencer one morning, he had his head down in his notebook and seemed discouraged. "Ms. Singer, I don't have a camera or film. I can't think of anything I want to do that doesn't involve photography. They will help create pictures for my poems." This conversation instigated a search through the school's technology center and photography lab to find Spencer a camera he could check out and borrow for his project. When Spencer finished shooting his photos, I took the slide film to a photo shop to get it developed. I continually reminded students of my high expectations for the final gallery and told them that, with their permission, I would invite other classes to witness and learn from their work. As students progressed on these projects,

I asked them every other class period during these final weeks to articulate the progress they were making through brief written reflections.

An example of a written reflection I created for this unit is "Teaching to Promote Change: A Game Plan" (see Handout 5.2).

Students used different strategies for mapping out and planning their projects. For his game plan, Nate wrote "I plan to get work done in the library today and at home. I will think of what I want to do and find info on it. I need to get to work. My mom and my dad will help me on it. I think I will need a pencil and colored pencils and a computer ink printer and keyboard, and, of course, my hands. Put them all together, and you will get a really good project. I hope!" Nate used this check-in as a way of rallying himself to accomplish the task at hand. He planned his final project around trying to reduce issues of discrimination at the local skateboard park. Margo wrote about her topic and her plans: "My issue is discrimination. I am going to write a proposal to the school officials here at Cleveland High School to gain permission to paint a mural on the school and hopefully have them pay for it! First, I will make a mock-up of the mural. I will paint one of the sections as a model. I am going to do this at home in my basement. Then I am going to use my computer at home to draft a proposal. I will probably have my mom read it and tell me what she thinks." Veronica mapped out her plan of progress by sketching a calendar and assigning specific tasks to each day. Emma wrote me a letter to share her plans:

Dear Ms. Singer,

My topic is diversity and tolerance in schools among students. I'm planning on putting together an art piece of a painting, using strong words or statements from magazines to use decoupage in the painting. I'm going to need poster board–sized paper, watercolors, decoupage, magazines, tissue paper, and a pencil. I want to watercolor a painting of three teenagers all with completely different personalities. Then, I will collage words that help display and explain my issue clearly.

I'm going to work on this in my basement at our large worktable. I plan to work on it over the next two weekends and hopefully, finish by the 3rd. I'm going to get feedback from my family before I turn it in, and I'd like to get feedback from you

Teaching to Promote Positive Change: A Game Plan

In the next ten days, you will create a final project. This project will teach a new way of seeing an issue that can promote positive change. On the day of the gallery, you will bring the following to class:

- Final Portfolio—organized with a table of contents and hole-punched
- Final Activism Project
- Artist Statement—typed and polished

In the space below, please share a game plan for how you will create, polish, and complete these requirements. Please tell me when you plan to get work done, where, what your process will be, who you will share feedback with or receive feedback from, what supplies you will need, how I can be of help to you, and any questions or concerns you have. There will be a writing workshop on artist statements.

Due Date: _____

on my artist statement. As of now, I don't have any questions or concerns, but if I do, I will definitely ask.

Thanks,

Emma

Kenzo used this check-in to start thinking about his topic. He was a bit behind and still needed to brainstorm. "First of all, I need to think of a topic. I want to choose something that is not too easy or boring. But if I do something too hard and big, it won't work because it would be too much to do in such a short amount of time. I am usually the type that leaves things to the last minute. I am going to do my best this time to work on this project a little every day. Easier said than done." Lisa used her written reflection to articulate her decision to change topics. "I think I want to change my topic. My old topic was how teens are stereotyped, but now after thinking about it, I think I want to do my final project on sweatshops and cheap labor. I saw this movie on TV during the summer, and the girl who played the lead in the movie worked at a sweatshop. My mom walked in while I was watching the movie and saw the girl working at the sweatshop, and then it went to a commercial. My mom then told me how she had worked at a sweatshop. And how she was treated unfairly and paid too little. I think my aunt also worked in a sweatshop too. I'll have to check. I can go online because I know there are sites about this issue." I encouraged students like Lisa to switch their topics even after they had started if they figured out another idea that appealed to them more. I told them that I would rather they work on something they were truly passionate about rather than just trying to finish an assignment. Lisa's choice to switch to a topic that touched her own life seemed like a good one because it renewed her interest and enthusiasm for the work.

Providing students with opportunities to write about their progress and plans again and again seemed to help them more clearly articulate and hone in on their interests. Mary described her intention to create a project about lack of funding for local libraries. "I wish to write a story about my experience with libraries. I will illustrate it with cool photos or collage. I hope to leave the reader understanding why it is that libraries have touched so many lives. I plan on starting this story over the week-end. I will have a copy on Tuesday that I would like to have you edit. I will also try to have my family edit my work too. In order to create positive change, I will send a copy of this story with a letter to my congressperson so that they may see why it is I believe that libraries need more funding. After I finish the story, I will decide on a way to illustrate it, either with drawings or collage." Sam used one of his reflections to express doubt about his project. "Honestly, my plan doesn't really work. My original plan was to do a piece of the final project every night, working on it toward perfection until the due date. I have planned on doing a series of political cartoons. I don't really believe I will be able to stick to my goals. I will probably be up until the early hours of the morning working on it at the last minute. I will start the drawings tonight." After reading Sam's words, I met with him and we brainstormed ways of making his political cartoon project more realistic for the amount of time he had until the final gallery. He decided to cut the amount of cartoons he would draw and to try to focus more in class.

This kind of goal setting and reflection seemed crucial to the success of the culminating project. Students only had a couple of weeks to design, create, and present these final projects; besides giving them class time to work, these check-ins served as a net to catch students who were struggling and as a way of showing students how taking a step-by-step and planned approach to their studies can help them succeed. Mary turned to me during class to tell me, "Ms. Singer, I'm stoked on all these check-ins. My mom's been nagging me forever to use a daily planner. Now, I see why. I'm going to start using my planner to make better plans for my homework."

Artist Statements

Along with the final project, I wanted students to write an explanation of their project's purpose so that an audience could read the reasoning behind the work. I thought that a written explanation of some kind would allow students to teach others about the issue they cared about. My closest friend, Jake, is a remarkable artist. He often calls me to share his artist description statements, which he posts with his latest work displayed in galleries. Here is an example of one of his recent artist statements, written in the third person to describe and promote his latest project:

First Print Available in a Limited-Edition Poster Series Highlighting Santa Barbara Landmarks

Artist Jake Early unveils his first image in a limited-edition series of hand printed serigraphs of Santa Barbara landmarks. The **Santa Barbara Courthouse** is the featured landmark on this initial print. Early, who illustrates and prints each serigraph by hand, will complete the series of 10 landmarks over the coming months. Editions are limited to only 100 prints and are available to the public at Drishti, 130 E. Canon Perdido St., Santa Barbara (across from the Presidio).

"I have an interest in public buildings and public gathering spaces and find a beauty in their ability to serve in utilitarian, civic and aesthetic functions," said Early. "These are the places that truly make Santa Barbara special, but are often overlooked or underappreciated in our day-to-day rush. I am proud of these places and feel compelled to 'show them off.'"

Serigraphs (or screenprints) are created using a series of screens—one for each color—to achieve their unique look and feel. Early illustrates each landmark by working from photographs and/or by sitting down at the site and simply drawing it. Once finished with the design, Early prints each image by hand in his studio. A trademark of Early's work is the use of metallic ink in every print he creates. Metallic inks are created by mixing powdered metals into a clear ink base prior to printing. These inks tend to pick up and reflect light, often changing the mood of the print throughout the day as the lighting conditions change.

Early won't reveal what landmark is next in the series, but does offer a hint by saying, "not every print I have in mind is a man-made structure. There are so many natural landmarks I think deserve attention. My goal with this project is to do the work I love, while I try to draw attention to some of the wonderful, local landmarks we all pass by in our daily lives."

After talking with Jake and gaining inspiration from his writing and paintings, I began thinking about artist statements as an authentic and creative writing genre to share with students. I love how this expository genre requires the artist to clearly and concisely articulate their purpose and process. Jake sent me a collection of artist statements from his own work as well as the work of other artists he admires to use as models to share with students. I introduced students to artist statements by telling them about Jake's screenprinting and by sharing examples of the statements he had written for gallery shows and press releases. I asked if students remembered reading or seeing artist statements in museums they had visited. I found and copied artist statements from the Portland Art Museum's recent exhibit. Then I explained how one of the requirements for the final activism project was to write a polished artist statement to accompany the presentation.

In a previous year's curriculum I included the artist statement as one of the requirements of a culminating project for a unit I called "The Passion Project." This unit gave seniors the opportunity to research, write, read, and teach others about a passion in their lives. For the final project in this unit, students took over the class for thirty minutes and taught their peers about their passions using creative and compelling teaching techniques as well as a visual project with an artist statement. I made copies of my seniors' work and used the artist statements as models with my ninth graders a year later. (For more information on "The Passion Project" see "Teaching from the Heart" [Singer and Hubbard 2003].)

I also shared Katie's artist statement with students, which was written her senior year to accompany a painting portraying her love of fly fishing:

Artist Statement

In a creek, cast one, nothing, cast two, still nothing and then the final cast, a rise. A fish flying through the air going after a feathered fly. The chase is on.

The Chase began as just a simple painting of a fish going after a fly connected to a line. As an avid fly fisherwoman, this idea for my painting came easily. Just a simple rainbow trout chasing a wooly bugger fly, nothing fancy. The hard part was finding meaning in my painting and to articulate the message I am sending through the paint. How do you find meaning from a fish chasing a fly?

As I created this simple painting, I began to notice something about why I enjoy fly-fishing so much. I love the chase. Just the simple joy of seeing a fish pick your fake fly out of hundreds of real ones and chase it through the air is exhilarating. While I was creating my art, I was thinking about the goals I want to achieve in my future life. I realized in my thinking that the chase of fly-fishing is like a chase in life. The only difference is that in life you are not chasing fish, you are chasing your goals.

When you finally catch that fish, it is a wonderful feeling, just like catching that goal. I hope everyone catches his or her "fish."

—*Katie Gray (fly fisher and artist)*

Katie's striking piece not only takes the reader into why she loves this sport, but it also describes fishing's rhythmic and meditative qualities and its connection to her aspirations.

After sharing multiple examples of these written statements with students, I asked them to begin drafting their own. Coco wrote her artist statement to accompany her final project about deforestation in Oregon.

The Dream and the Reality

Watercolors on watercolor paper
Have you ever driven over the mountains to the coast surrounded by majestic Oregon pine trees? Did you ever notice that just behind the layer of trees by the side of the road is a vast graveyard of stumps, of dried and fallen branches bereft or wildlife, shade, and water? If not, take a closer look next time you take a drive to the coast. This is the real status of our "beautiful Oregon old growth forests." Despite what the developers, the loggers, and the politicians want you to think, Oregon is not a state filled with breathtaking wilderness and life. Although this pristine beauty survives in some areas, most are being eaten away by the lumber industry.

For this project, I wanted to make paintings that would be easily recognizable, while also having a message that registered inside the viewer. Although logging and deforestation are worldwide problems, I hope to get a simpler idea across that strikes closer to home. In these two pictures, I want people to see images that remind them of things they have already seen just a few hours' drive from Portland. By using something this recognizable, I hope I can make an impact in the way you view the state of your surroundings, and hopefully your interest in this issue will grow.

Figure 5.1: Leigh's final gallery project drawing about the need for school funding

From this project I hope that you, the viewer, will walk away at least a little more thoughtful and a little more observant about our forests. Don't just look at outward appearances (i.e., the trees left standing at the side of the road). Instead, look past the outward layer, and find the truth. In this case, the clear-cut wasteland on the other side.

Here is the drawing and a selection of an essay from Laurie's remarkable final project, about the need for increased school funding (see Figure 5.1).

Budget Cuts

When I was in elementary school, there was a great music teacher there named Mr. Stone. Twice a week, every class got to go sing, dance, play the tambourines, and just have fun in his class. My elementary school P.E. class was similar. It was a place where we could get up and move around, play games, and stay physically fit. There was a wonderful teacher for that class, too: Mrs. Huntley. She had won a bronze medal in the Olympics for the high jump. It was so fun to go to those classes after sitting and watching teachers write on overheads all day. But by the time I reached fifth grade, the music, P.E., and art programs had been taken away from my school because of budget cuts in Portland Public Schools and throughout Oregon. That was a boring year for me. I felt a lot like the girl in my picture: bored, antsy, and thinking about more interesting things I could be doing with art and music and movement.

During the ten years I have been enrolled in Portland Public Schools, it seems like every year there are fewer extracurricular classes offered. These classes are crucial for a decent education and they are necessary to add some variety to students' days. These courses are so different than English, Math, and Social Studies, and therefore provide a wonderful break that enables pupils to concentrate better. Dropping course offerings is certainly not the only result of budget cuts. Teachers are fired and class sizes go up and up. It is a lot easier to learn when the teacher can give enough attention to every student, but that is not possible with huge classes. The janitorial staff has also been cut drastically. There is not a lot of emphasis on the importance of a janitor's job. When the janitors get fired, there is a big difference in the quality of my school environment. The dirt and garbage accumulates in classrooms, bathrooms, and hallways, making for a very unpleasant and smelly learning space.

It seems to me that many people think that as long as students are passing the state tests, they are doing just fine. When the money is tight, all effort is put into just having students learn the bare minimum. Budget cuts are slowly making our district's schools bleak and boring places, which is what I was hoping to illustrate with my picture. Finding enjoyment in school is important for students to get the most out of their education. I do not know why the state's funds are so tight that so much money has to be taken out of the schools. This needs to change. There must be some alternative. For example, if taxes were raised just a little bit and these funds were given to schools, I am sure it would make a huge difference. I wish the voters of our state, or whoever is in charge, could understand that.

The Final Gallery

On the last class of the school year, students arrived at my class-room door forty-five minutes before the morning bell with posters, paintings, collages, mobiles, CDs and tapes, photographs, slides, poetry, political cartoons, and other creative activism projects. I set up the room with tables and chairs in a circle and asked students to find a space to display their activism projects as if the room were transformed into an art gallery. I reminded the class to post their artist statements next to their projects. Students were beaming with excitement. Paul said, "Ms. Singer, I worked on this for two days and two nights. I haven't slept at all. I think it's going to be good." Students gathered around one another's gallery spaces to share their work. When the bell rang, I told the class the plan for their final day together. Each student had time to share their proj-ects, read artist statements aloud, and provide details about their passion for their particular activism issue.

Coco began her gallery presentation by holding up her water-color paintings contrasting two forests: one that had been clear-cut and another that had been preserved. She read from her artist statement. Erik shared a poster of his photographs taken from around the school showing the impact of budget cuts on the school environment. In his statement, he explained:

> I took these pictures to show the damage that thoughtless peo-ple can do to a building. All the damage and mess that people make has to be cleaned up or repaired, but this costs money that the school district doesn't have. . . . With the decrease in fund-ing for schools, students need to look around and take care of what we have. Without the custodians working, this place will quickly turn into a disgusting dump and we need to do our part to keep our school as clean as we can.

Mary wrote a narrative telling of her connection to the public libraries in Portland and how they sparked her interest in reading:

Untitled
by Mary (Ninth Grade)

I stopped at the light at 39th and Taylor. I pressed the button to let me cross the street. When the light turned green, I quickly rode across the street, and up to the bike rack that sits outside the Belmont Public Library. I locked my bike and helmet to the rack, grabbed the books I had to return out of my basket, and checked my back pocket for my wallet. I walked up the ramp to the door. When I tried to open the door, it was locked. Then I remembered that the library is closed on Mondays.

I went around to the back of the building and dropped my books in the return slot. "At least," I thought, "I won't get charged for late fees." Then I pedaled back home trying to think about reasons the library had to close every Monday. This is not the normal schedule. It is due to a lack of funding that the library is not open every day. So I began to think about ways I could help bring funding back to the public libraries that I love so much.

I remember the first "chapter book" I ever read. I found it at the Belmont Library in the children's section. *The Fledgling*, by Jane Langston, is still one of my favorite books. After that, I read almost every other one of Ms. Langston's books that I could find. Her books were about a family that lived in Massachusetts and all of their adventures and mysteries that they solved. It's funny, when I find an author I like, I read all of his or her books and then I'm on to a new author. In that tradition, my next author after Langston was John Bellairs. He wrote mysteries with many reoccurring characters, just like Ms. Langston. The first of Mr. Bellairs' books that I read was *The Doom of the Haunted Opera*, which is a chilling mystery about an opera written a hundred years ago. The alleged great grandson of the composer comes to the small town where the story takes place and asks the high school band to perform. But the main character and his friends discover that when the last note of the opera is played, the composer will come back to life and control the world.

Without public libraries, I would not have found these books. I would not have found my sanctuary that is reading. I remember reading in books about characters' trips to the library, where they could only check out three books at a time. I am happy that we are now allowed to check out as many books as we want. However, I personally try to just get as many books as my arms can hold. Sometimes, on long summer days, I will ride my bike to the library and just sit and read there. I don't even bother to check out a book. I just love to read in that space. I have been to the library so many times now. I know where to find almost everything. They could probably hire me as a reference librarian.

I have been to the library so often to get help with school projects or questions, but now it's time for me to help the libraries. There needs to be more money to hire librarians and to support these wonderful hideaways. Some of the books I have checked out lately have been tattered and falling apart. Why? Because there is not enough money to fix or replace them. I, for one, want to change this. I plan to send a letter to both my congressman and the newspaper about this issue. I hope that you will do the same so that we may return our libraries to their original splendor and other young readers will fall in love with books pulled from the library's shelves.

Mary read this narrative along with her artist statement as her gallery presentation. She also included the letters she wrote to the congressman and newspaper on her final poster.

Margo painted an incredible image about discrimination and hate at high school. Her goal was to paint a mural on the side of the school. So she created a proposal for this project and then painted one section of her final mural image (see Figure 5.2). She wrote a poem to accompany this painting:

Hate Does Not See
by Margo (Ninth Grade)
Hate does not see
A mother and daughter
Hate does not see
A little boy lost
Hate does not see
All the pain that it causes
Hate does not see
All the people it hurts
Hate does not see
Individual faces
Hate does not see
The lives it has claimed
So take in your heart
A different person
An individual
And try to understand
We are all different and
Unique in a way
But together we stand
And have this to say

Figure 5.2: Margo's mural painting about tolerance

Segregation is wrong
Discrimination is out-dated
So love our differences
And give the blindness of hate
A new sight to see
A human wave
All difference and special
United as one
In an effort for peace.

Emma painted an image (see Figure 5.3) depicting the pain that arises when people are discriminated against in high school. She wrote the following artist statement to accompany her painting:

Figure 5.3: Emma's painting about discrimination in high school

Down the Halls of High School
Emma (Ninth Grade)

Canvas, Acrylics, Teen People *magazine cutouts, Mod-Podge*
As I walk down the halls of my high school, I pass the preppy cheerleader, the skater, the jock, and the quiet intellectual. There are the class clowns, the brainiacs, and the wallflowers standing to the side and watching behind expressionless eyes.

How can this be? People have so many different personalities and these titles are all one-dimensional. The cheerleader may also be an "A" student who starred in the last school play. The skater may be the next Picasso in art class who, last Friday, made the winning basket for the school team. The wallflower may be the lead singer in the garage band and a state champion in downhill skiing.

The media has helped encourage these kinds of stereotypes through movies and magazines. People use these stereotypes as an excuse to discriminate against each other. Intolerance of people with different personalities and personal styles can continue unnecessarily throughout our lives. We exclude others because they are different than us. This discrimination can take place because of little things, such as clothing and haircuts.

It is important for schools to teach tolerance toward others. This can be achieved by something as simple as sitting by different people in class occasionally or working with people outside of your circle of friends. I am committed to working toward reaching out to all different kinds of people with varying interests. I hope you will be committed to this work too!

In the last part of the class, students had time to circle around the room—as they would in any art gallery—and observe the projects. I laid out blank pieces of paper next to each project so that students could give one another positive feedback. The gallery format and artist statements emphasized the individual creativity in student work and the community. When people go to an art gallery, they interact with the art and reflect on what it means to them. This was not a final presentation for me as the teacher— rather, it was a celebration of the three-month unit for the students to share together.

Conclusion

This curriculum created a foundation and tools necessary for students to launch out of the classroom and into the world of activism. Equally important, this work provided bridges from one student to another. They learned compassion for each other, not just for causes outside of themselves. One of the most articulate students became an ally for one of her peers who struggled with communication. A shy and introverted student, Spencer gained confidence through the support and respect of his classmates. He ended the year by sharing his slide-show project about overcoming hate, along with the following poem:

Untitled
by Spencer
You may not like us
We may not like you
No matter what you think
Or how we feel
We are the future

Today is the day we fight the battle
The battle for pride, love, and trust
The future is in us

We will do our job
Cleaning up the mess of today
We don't need these problems
The hate or the mistakes

As you dream of tomorrow
Remember your thoughts of today
Look into the sky up up and away

You have your fears
You have your doubts
But you must remember
We are tomorrow's leaders.

Spencer received an ovation and numerous written accolades from his classmates after his final presentation. Students supported one another's ideas, edited one another's pieces, and witnessed both challenges and successes.

References

Hoose, P. 2001. *We Were There, Too! Young People in U.S. History.* New York: Farrar, Straus & Giroux.

Singer, J., and R. Hubbard. 2003. "Teaching from the Heart: Guiding Adolescent Writers to Literate Lives." *Journal of Adolescent and Adult Literacy* 46 (4): 326–38.

6   Discoveries, Lingering Questions, and Conclusions

> Sometimes we convince ourselves that the
> unnoticed gestures of "insignificant" peo-
> ple mean nothing. It's not enough to recy-
> cle our soda cans; we must stop global
> warming now. Since we can't stop global
> warming now, we may as well not recycle
> our soda cans. It's not enough to be our
> best selves; we have to be Gandhi. And
> yet when we study the biographies of our
> heroes, we learn that they spent years in
> preparation, doing tiny, decent things . . .
>
> —Danusha Veronica Goska,
> "Political Paralysis"

How can the work we do every day in language arts classes connect to larger issues that lie beyond our classroom walls? How
may the lives and activism of people such as Arundhati Roy,
Nelson Mandela, Harriet Tubman, Eleanor Roosevelt, Jane
Goodall, and many others feel personally inspiring to students?
How can they grow to feel that their reading, writing, and actions
will make meaningful, positive change in their own lives and
communities? This three-month integrated unit on activism was
an effort to share the work of successful activists with students so
they could understand how this kind of positive action is possible in their own lives.

Instead of trying to persuade students to follow any particular
activism agenda, this project lets students experience the power of
knowing how to act on something they personally care about. I
have the hope that this will serve them well in their futures when
faced with issues or events in their communities that matter to

them. When confronted with challenging circumstances, instead of thinking "there's nothing I can do to make this better," they will know clearly how to respond in informed and significant ways. The choice to respond or take action will always be their own.

A tension exists for an educator between teaching what you believe and leading students closer to articulating and formulating their own beliefs. This tension is accentuated when inviting political or pedagogical material to become the focus of a curriculum. One could easily argue that all curriculum choices are political in some way. If I choose to teach Alice Walker's *The Color Purple*, then I choose to enter a conversation about issues of oppression, racism, and slavery. If I decide to teach from an anthology of stories that excludes women's voices, then I am making another political choice. The political nature of curricula is not news in the field of English education. Making the decision to focus on activism meant that I did not have time to teach other texts that I love, such as Shakespeare's *Romeo and Juliet* or Rudolfo Anaya's *Bless Me Ultima*. Even though some texts were set aside to make room for this curriculum, the books students chose to read for this unit are significant and sophisticated.

I realize that in many departments, schools, and districts, teachers do not have the freedom to push aside certain texts and replace them with others. In these times of standardization and accountability, making changes to a curriculum can feel like a risk. I maintain that the skills that need to be addressed in high school language arts courses can be taught and practiced through an innovative social justice curriculum. In this curriculum, students wrote and revised narrative and expository essays as well as poetry, researched using primary and secondary sources, read sophisticated texts, increased vocabulary, presented publicly, and published their work.

Lingering Questions: Teaching a Diverse Population

There are conversations that would not have happened in the same way if this class had been designated as an honors class or regular class. The range of experiences and opinions varied widely. Teaching an untracked class provided challenges. I designed curricula and teaching strategies to address the wide range of my students' skills, interests, and experiences. Still I am left with some lingering questions about students who struggled. Out of forty-five students in my first and second periods, two boys did not complete the final project and one girl completed no work throughout the unit until the final gallery project. Nate, the struggling reader and writer, made progress over the course of the year in his reading and writing fluency. He read his book of choice, *Life in Prison*, and participated in our daily reading and writing workshops. He often shared stories from the text with other students and he often completed pieces of projects. However, when it came time for him to write the article about an activist in his book, he plagiarized the paper. When I asked him to rewrite the paper if he wanted to receive credit for the assignment, he unfortunately chose not to rewrite this piece and did not complete the final gallery project. Ben has severe, untreated Attention Deficit Disorder and exhibits a wide variety of inappropriate class behaviors. He is seriously delayed in reading and writing, perhaps due to his inability to focus. He often began pieces of writing and then could not get past an opening sentence, never completing any assignments. As an educator, I often fixate on the students who are not succeeding. I ask myself, "What could I do to modify curricula and support my students' learning needs?" I try to reflect on my teaching choices to understand how I could have reached these students. I have also learned that students are complex and that their home lives and years of falling through the cracks influence what happens in my classroom. Still, if I could live this year of teaching over again, I would have fought for more support for these students through counselors, the Educational Resource Center, and their parents. I would have tried to incorporate even more cooperative learning activities and more structured curricula modifications to increase these students' participation.

Looking back on the unit and thinking of ways to strengthen it for future years, I would have invited parents to the final gallery. Most parents would be impressed with their child's work and supportive of their efforts, and their presence would have enriched the gallery event. In the future, parents will be included. Having parents present will provide important "ears" to hear the students and witness the remarkable work of these young adults.

Expanding Definitions of Activism

When I began brainstorming ideas for this curriculum, I thought about what it means to be an activist. At the time, I had an image in my head of my mother as a college student. My mom went to college at the University of California–Berkeley during the free speech movement in the 1960s. I grew up hearing her tell stories of the impact of student protests on national policy and values. As a child, whenever I thought about activism I pictured my mom standing alongside thousands of her classmates demonstrating for civil rights. Now, years later, as a high school teacher interested in creating curricula for my students to understand and explore the work of activists, I realize how my understanding of what counts as activism was narrow when I was growing up. Through integrated and long-term projects, my students created wonderful activism projects connected to their own interests. Through my students' creative letters to congressional representatives about school budget cuts, mural paintings of tolerance, community gardens, photo essays about clear-cutting, and websites about stem cell research and animal rights, my definition of activism work has shifted. I learned through their work and experiences how positive social change is created in a multitude of ways, through both large and small acts. Time spent with my students studying activists helped me expand my own definition and perception of what it means to work toward change. One of the biggest lessons I learned, both as an individual interested in activism and as a teacher, is that this kind of careful and in-depth learning takes time.

Stirring Up Justice allowed students to explore an issue in depth that resonated with their own experiences and interests. This teaching and curricular choice was intentional and connected to my pedagogy as a teacher committed to social justice education. Nadine Dolby writes, "Democracy cannot be imposed as a set of principles coming from above to which individuals must subscribe. It must start within the core of people's dreams and desires and from where people are" (2003, 276).

Jenna's words, taken from her final self evaluation of the project, show the continuing impact of Stirring Up Justice:

After reading about this wonderful person [Holocaust rescuer Irene Opdyke] it really makes me see the world differently. It makes me think of what I want to do that will work to influence positive social change in the world. Irene taught me that you really don't have to listen and follow the rules all the time. She taught me that you have to follow your heart and let it take you to that special place of being a social activist.

Jenna's quote reinforces how social justice teaching does not end with the bell in June. Students began projects that will continue. Matt plans to expand and update his website on stem cell research. Margo's gallery project was a painting that will become part of a larger mural design for the school. She plans to write a proposal to the art department and administration that outlines how she will design and complete her mural by the end of her senior year. After creating a poster and a wealth of talking points on the issue of animal testing and mistreatment, Erin has become part of the larger animal rights movement and has taken part in teach-ins and political rallies.

The students' passion and commitment to their ongoing projects demonstrated both political imagination and an ability to use literacy to exercise agency in the world. Not only did the students have grounded definitions of social activism, but they also grew to see themselves as individuals capable of influencing real and effective change in their lives. Through their participation in a classroom community that treated reading and writing as political acts, students experienced fundamental changes in themselves, which were reflected in their work. Students show that they have the power to be a part of a generation that uses reading and writing to help improve their lives.

Lastly, I have immense gratitude to my students for allowing me to engage with them in my own exciting and challenging activism project through the creation and implementation of this curriculum and book. I had the unique experience of arriving to class each day and seeing and listening to the development and oral and written expression of the individual passionate concerns of the students in my class. Their wholehearted participation gave me the greatest faith in the ability of individuals to improve the world we live in.

References

Anaya, R. 1994. *Bless Me Ultima*. New York: Warner.

Dolby, N. 2003. "Popular Culture and Democratic Practices." *Harvard Educational Review* 73 (3): 258–84.

Goska, D.V. 2005. "Political Paralysis." *Sun Magazine* 347: 14–16.

Shakespeare, W. 2000. *Romeo and Juliet*, ed. J. Levenson. New York: Oxford University Press.

Walker, A. 1992. *The Color Purple*. New York: Harcourt.

Appendix 1

Unit Timeline

Week (1–11)	Curriculum Presented	Student Tasks
1	Children's Books on Activism (see Handout 1.1)	Read and respond to children's books in children's book workshop
		Write a reflection about children's book workshop
	Famous Activist Quotes	Respond to quotes in a short writing warm-up
	Sample Narratives	Write a rough draft of a narrative about an experience with injustice
2	Models of Children's Book Illustrations	Illustration workshop: students create illustrations for their stories of injustice
	Minilesson: Audience	Revise narratives in small groups
	Minilesson: Leads	Revise lead for narrative
	Articles About Activists	Read the collection of articles as an introduction to activist work
3	Minilesson on Descriptive Language	Revise narratives to add description
	Deadline	Turn in working draft of narrative for teacher feedback
	Social Activism Book List (see Handout 2.2)	Read list and browse through sample books in class
	Minilesson on Revision	Receive narratives with teacher's comments and work on revising with editing suggestions
4	**Deadline**	Arrive in class with activism book of choice (if unprepared there are books available in the classroom)
		Revise narratives and work on illustrations
		Share books and write about selection process
	Text-to-Self Minilesson	Read books in class (2–3 times a week for 3½ weeks) and for home-work
		Write about first impressions of the books

5	**Deadline**	Turn in edited narratives and illustrations
		Share pieces of final narratives and illustrations with the class
	Sample Timeline	Create a timeline of major events in activism book of choice
	Turning Point Workshop (Collection of Writing About Turning Points)	Short essay on a turning point in the life of the activist in book of choice
6	Minilesson: Inner Voice	Read silently in class and record questions and reactions to text
		Write rough draft of activist article
	Minilesson: Background Information	Collect background info about activist for article
7	Minilesson: Embedding Quotes	Collect quotes to include in article
	Minilesson: Successful Endings	Write multiple endings and choose one for activism article
	Deadline	Finish activism books of choice
	Minilesson: Giving Good Feedback	Peer review for activism articles
		Book hunt and book hunt reflection letter
8	**Deadline**	Turn in activism articles
	Minilesson: Brainstorming	Brainstorm topic for personal activism projects
		Write a game plan for activism project
	Model Activism Projects	Work on final activism projects in class (2–3 times a week for 2 weeks)
	Minilesson: Writing a Proposal	Write a rough draft of a proposal for activism project
9	Songs of Protest Workshop	Students listen to and write responses to songs of protest
	Minilesson: Library Search	Go to library to research activism topic
	Deadline	Students bring in lyrics for songs of protest and share as a class
10	Share Collection of Artist Statements	Write rough draft of artist statement and share
		Organize unit portfolio

	Deadline	Turn in artist statement for teacher feedback
11	**Deadline**	Final activism gallery: share and turn in projects
	Deadline	Write a final reflection letter and turn in with final portfolio

Appendix 2

Portfolio Table of Contents

1.

2.

3.

4.

5.

6.

7.

8.

9.

10.

11.

12.

13.

14.

15.

16.

17.

18.

19.

20.

21.

22.

23.

24.

25.

26.

27.

28.